THE UNTOLD COST OF PUTTING MISSION FIRST

BRINGING THEM HOME

ANNA PAULINA LUNA

Post Hill Press

A POST HILL PRESS BOOK
ISBN: 978-1-63758-018-9
ISBN (eBook): 978-1-63758-019-6

Bringing Them Home:
The Untold Cost of Putting Mission First

While many of the people, places, and situations described are based on true events, many names and identifying details have been changed to protect the privacy of the people involved. Although every effort has been made to ensure that the personal advice present within this book is useful and appropriate, the author and publisher do not assume and hereby disclaim any liability to any person choosing to employ the guidance offered in this book.

Post Hill Press
New York • Nashville
posthillpress.com

Published in the United States of America
1 2 3 4 5 6 7 8 9 10

In the United States military, there are several divisions of special operations. Only a handful of those in the military will ever be able to say they belong to this elite group. This book is dedicated to any woman who has ever loved one of these men, as well as all the military spouses past and present, and the friends and loved ones who never came home from deployment.

"I never saw a wild thing sorry for itself.
A small bird will drop frozen dead from a bough
without ever having felt sorry for itself."

D.H. Lawrence

CONTENTS

CHAPTER 1

Enlistment and the South

I THINK IT'S SAFE TO SAY that at nineteen years old, you think you're invincible. Growing up with palm trees and sunshine gave me a Los Angeles flare. I had grown up with salty air and the Hollywood sign in sight. Fake boobs, fake smiles, and fake IDs were a reality. I was at the center of it all. I could have done anything, so I did. My life hadn't always been a walk on the beach. I'd come from a broken family. The people closest to me had struggled with abuse, drug addiction, and poverty. I didn't want that life for myself, so when a military recruiter showed up in my life talking about honor and service and the promise of money for college, I was sold. Dreams of the American flag and pride in my country fueled my fire. I desired change.

I showed up to MEPS, the military entrance processing station, at 110 pounds, in a designer coat I had saved up for. I could have just walked out of a couture photo shoot, for all they knew. I worked the camera with a confident grin and signed my life away for the next six years.

"You did what?" my mother screamed. She was not pleased.

"I joined the Air Force," I said. "…and I'm leaving today." It wasn't exactly the best breakfast conversation.

"I'm telling Dad." She looked at me defiantly. Her threat was about as effective as a piece of paper to stop a bullet. I waited patiently as she dialed Dad's number. "Do you know what your daughter did? She joined the military. She is leaving today. Do you hear?" I could hear indistinct freaking out on the other line. "This is not my fault. It's yours, always putting ideas…" She walked into the next room. They had been pretty good about not fighting recently, but I guess I blew that one. Eventually, her murmurs calmed, and she returned to hand the phone to me.

"Here."

"Hello?" I was a little nervous, but I also knew there was nothing that could stop me now.

"So, this is what you've decided for yourself?" my dad asked.

"Yes." I was too scared to say anything else.

He let out a worrisome sigh. "Fine, but you need to take care of yourself. Don't let them steal your fire."

"I won't."

"Give the phone back to your mom. We still have some things to discuss."

I handed the phone to my mom. She swept it out of my hand with a pouty look on her face. She turned on her heel and marched into the other room. I smiled to myself. Even with a nineteen-year-old as a daughter, she was still such a young soul.

The United States was right in the middle of the global war on terror, and there I was, getting ready to leave for the military. I had grown up a tomboy, climbing roofs and torturing the neighborhood boys. I dreaded wearing dresses all together. When I hit high school, I grew up, if that's what you want to call it. I started wearing makeup and wearing skinny jeans. School cliques in LA were relentless. If you didn't have perfect everything, you were nothing and yet, all of this seemed so superficial. On the inside, though, I was still that girl climbing roofs, wanting to be an FBI agent like Agent Dana Scully from *The X-Files*. I had it all figured out. I would use the military to pay for my schooling. It was going to be a piece of cake. A walk in the park. I had beauty and brains; that meant the world was mine, or so I thought.

In fact, I showed up to basic military training as a vegetarian and a model with bright red Dolce & Gabbana reading glasses. "Oh, look what we have here," my drill instructor said with a sickening smile. "Little Miss Gucci." *They're Dolce*, I thought, but I was smart enough to know not to talk back to a drill instructor. My military-issued glasses never came in the mail, and every single drill instructor in Lackland Air Force Base never let me live it down. My revenge was my own black-market trade. I would help the girls in my dorm with perfectly manicured brows, and in return, they would fold my clothes, shine my shoes, and make my bed. It was a surprisingly good business. Little Miss Gucci was the leader of the underground eyebrow market. I don't know which I am prouder of, my black-market enterprise or that I graduated with an honor graduate ribbon. Granted, I was still the best at all of the above tasks, but why bother when we could collectively work together to get it done faster? Priorities, including eyebrows, are a must. That was at least one thing my recruiter was actually right about; basic training goes by in the blink of an eye.

My graduation ceremony was nice. It was a formal sort of thing. I got to wear my pristine uniform, with my cool hat and fancy name tag. I had become accustomed to having my hair slicked back so tight that it couldn't hold a candle to Botox. I had also learned the art of perfecting my makeup, all according to military standards, of course. It was a sigh of relief. I was done, and I was moving on.

"Gucci," my drill instructor said in a dad voice. My eyes widened. I didn't know which was more shocking, the fact that he wasn't yelling or that he was going dad-mode on me. "Don't you dare get married in tech school. They're going to try to marry you, but don't do it. You're a smart girl. You got a lot to offer. Keep your head on straight and you'll do well. When the right man comes along, you'll know." I tried to smile gratefully, but I don't think it came across because he let out a thick "Ha!" and walked away. I got on the bus for tech school and took one last look at the place I had learned to hate, but there was a strange tightness in my chest. I tried to brush it off. When my bus started to pull away, I saw my instructor wave goodbye.

As the bus pulled away, something hit me. Unlike some of the other girls, I was never told that I had a choice in choosing my job. When I showed up to my recruiter, I know for a fact he took one look at me and thought "easy target." What I later found out is recruiters are notorious for saying and doing anything to meet their enlistment numbers. Granted, not all are bad, but Sergeant Lime, my recruiter, told me that if I didn't take the job he gave me, I could not join the military.

Obviously, I wanted to join, so without questioning him, I signed on the dotted line.

That was a huge mistake. I quickly remembered the conversations with a few of my friends in my basic training flight. Most of us already knew where we would be going for our job training, aka technical school, but the difference between me and them was they had a choice and I had been lied to.

Had I been able to choose my job, I would have technically known where I would be going and what to potentially expect. The military has pretty much any job that exists in the civilian world from post office to cooks, to construction, to attorneys. Depending on what job you get, you are then sent to that particular technical school. So, as I sat on the bus, headed to Keesler Air Force Base in Mississippi, it occurred to me that there was a lot I didn't know, ESPECIALLY about the military, and at that moment, I got really nervous.

The bus was pleasant. A lovely downgrade from Greyhound. After the first couple of hours, I started to envy the girls who got to take a plane to their tech schools. The bus made its first stop after four hours at a ma-and-pa place in a quaint backwoods town. This was the first time I had left Los Angeles and to my amazement, instead of the relentless traffic and constant commotion, there was something sweet about the sleepiness of this town. Since I had entered the military, a few things had changed about me, one of those being my choice in diet. Yep, you guessed it: this LA girl now ate meat. I ordered a warm bowl of chicken soup. It was creamy and savory, with just the right ratio of chicken and noodles to vegetables. Either I was starving or I had been a complete idiot for the last few years by not eating meat. It was A-MAZING.

The restaurant was empty, but you could tell by the worn-down, torn seats that it had seen its golden days. The smell of old leather and home cooking reminded me a lot of some of the movies I had watched growing up. Something about it was almost surreal. Compared to where I grew up, seeing this made me realize that LA wasn't all that glamorous. As we got back onto the bus and headed to our next stop, it hit me. My skin started getting clammy, and the cold shivers came. Dreaded food poisoning. If you want to know what it feels like to be on a long-distance bus with food poisoning, don't. I don't even remember arriving at Keesler Air Force Base. Somewhere on the way to Mississippi, I lost consciousness and my dorm roommate took care of me. She must have been about twenty-three at the time. By the time I started to get better, she had already left for her new base, and I was never able to tell her thank you. I tried to track her down, but nothing came of it. By the time I got an email at my first duty station and was even able to look her up, I found out that her last name, at least in the Air Force, was pretty common.

Keesler was a fairly new base. Four years prior, Hurricane Katrina had blown through, leaving devastation in her wake. Even then, the city was still in the process of rebuilding itself. Only two good things came from Keesler. One was Waffle House. My dorm-mate dragged me there, saying that if I never drank sweet tea, I never lived. So that's where I lost it, my sweet tea virginity, and man, was it good. Waffle House isn't the classiest place, but it was good! I was hooked on grits. I knew these types of places would never survive in the calorie-counting city of LA, but in the South? What the hell are calories anyways? The only thing you should care about is what you can't see: Jesus.

The other good thing was Nick, a combat controller and good friend, who later introduced me to the man who I would end up marrying. Keesler hosted a Special Olympics tournament every year. They place a Special Olympian in the care of a service member during the competitions. That year, my Olympian was a competitive swimmer. As I brought her to her event, there he was, standing at the opposite end of the pool, timing my athlete. He was the typical tall, handsome "hunk" type that all of my dorm-mates had a crush on. We clicked right away. We had a common love for fitness, food, and dogs. And if that is not enough commonality, we even had the same last name. Ironically enough, it turned out that we were related somewhere down the line, which to my relief, put Nick in the safe "friend zone." I had missed my guy friends and realized very quickly with the military that with the male-to-female ratio, platonic friendships were typically taken out of context.

Tech school was only a few months long. I didn't have much time to socialize, but I did eventually end up figuring out what my drill instructor meant about the marriage thing. The military lifestyle is hard on relationships in general. Whether you are dating a civilian or another service member, distance is the number one relationship killer. At tech school, everyone finds out where their first duty assignment is. And many young military couples get married in hopes of being stationed together, or at least near each other, as if that is a perfectly sane reason for committing your life to someone.

As a result, there is a very high number of young marriages, but there is an equally high divorce rate. Maybe that is what is ruining the marriage statistic in the United States? I managed to make it out of tech school unscathed and with only two serious marriage proposals. Both were from guys who were trying to convince me that it was for purposes of "taking my fate into my own hands" regarding where I was going to get stationed. I happily declined. I had already given up my fate when I enlisted.

Prior to leaving tech school, I met with Nick for dinner one night and told him to stay in touch. Luckily for us, this was at the start of the Facebook era. Mind you, the only reason I even had a Facebook was because of my ex, and I hadn't been on in some time, but I ended up listening to Nick and added him before I left. Nick would always babble about his job, and frankly, I had no idea what a combat controller was, except that those poor guys had to run around everywhere on base. I would catch them from time to time running around with a damn telephone pole or a big ass rock. I didn't even bother asking Nick what they did. I just let my eyes glaze over after a while as I became lost in my own thoughts.... *Why the hell do they carry a telephone pole?*

My last day at Keesler was bittersweet. I was excited to get off base and have a bit of freedom back, but I was dreading the fact that I got orders to Whiteman Air Force Base. Whiteman is located in the small town of Knob Noster, Missouri. If that doesn't tell you why I was dreading going there, I don't know what will. So, I packed my duffle bag, took a cab to the airport, and headed back home for two weeks before going to my first duty assignment.

CHAPTER 2

Lawn Decorations

MY FIRST DUTY ASSIGNMENT WAS in the middle of nowhere. It was almost as if the people at Headquarters who determined the assignments had folded a map of the United States in half and then in half again, and where smack-dab Middle America was is where they decided to send me. There I was, a young city chick from Los Angeles, in the ass crack of America. The most grass I had ever seen was probably at Santa Monica Park, and now, I was staring at miles and miles of cornfields and Foster's Chicken Farms. Driving up to the base, all I could think about was the scene from *The Texas Chainsaw Massacre*.

The town outside the base was called Knob Noster. I remember taking a very hard look at the name and for the life of me, all I could think about is the fact that it sounded like a rare STD. Knob Noster has a total population of 1,200 people, according to the last census, although I was pretty sure the number was old and did not account for people passing away. My only hope was in another air traffic controller in my unit, Emily.

She was from a small town about twenty miles from base. I always thought she was lucky, but she despised the fact that she was stationed a skip away from her hometown. Maybe it was just my homesickness kicking in, but I envied how she could see her family whenever she wanted. I hoped my family was doing okay. You don't get the full story through phone receivers and computer screens.

The silence was the most shocking. I was used to cars honking, sirens, and people shouting on their phones. Going to sleep with nothing but the sound of crickets was harder than I imagined. The country life was new to me.

The only bar in town had regular line dancing competitions. I could no longer use my fake ID from LA. With only one bar, the chances of running into my supervisor were more than likely. Even in the restaurants around the base, you could find someone with cowboy boots lighting one up. Probably Marlboro. Seemed American enough. In LA, smoking indoors meant losing your license to do business. Small Town, USA, was something else, but it was growing on me. The smell of cut, dried grass. The musty, full smell of cattle. The click-clacks of boots instead of heels. On weekends, Emily and I would go to her parents' farm to ride horses.

I'd never been to a real farm before. By that, I mean not Knott's Berry Farm and not the touristy ones on the outskirts of Southern California. I had browsed through a few of the *Country Home and Garden* magazines at the local Walmart, the only place to shop in a fifty-square-mile radius. My expectations were high. I expected rolling green pastures and white picket fences. Like a scene from a Laura Ingalls Wilder book. I tried to decide which I liked more: the colonial-style mansions with fading white paint and antique furniture or the cozy style farmhouses with their large covered porches and circular, golden lawn decorations. Each had a charm of its own.

As we got closer to her parents' farm, I noticed the same lawn decorations. "Your farm is gorgeous," I told Emily. I was glad I had worn an old pair of tennis shoes. I hadn't yet convinced myself to buy a pair of boots. I didn't know how willing I was to let go of my city-slicker trappings.

"Awe, thanks. It's nothing special really," Emily said. I guess you can get comfortable with anything, beauty included. I couldn't decide if it was a good thing or a bad thing.

"I really like your lawn ornaments," I said, trying to liven the mood. "They're just like the ones I've seen in the magazines!"

"What in the Lord's name are you talkin' about?" she asked.

I pointed to the circular, golden lawn ornaments. "Those big things all over your lawn. They add so much character to your farm." She burst out laughing. The car swerved. She was shaking with laughter so much that I feared for our lives. "What?" I asked. I had no idea what was so hilarious. Her face was turning bright red and tears were forming in her blue eyes. She reminded me of Violet from *Charlie and the Chocolate Factory*, except Emily was turning into a tomato.

"Honey," she said when she had finally calmed down enough to get words out, "those ain't lawn decorations. That's our livelihood. They're hay bales." She started again. I hoped she would get a stomachache later on. I wondered how it was physically possible to laugh that much and not explode from a lack of oxygen. How was I supposed to know? The only hay bales I'd ever seen were at pumpkin patches, and they were rectangular and itchy. My mom had made me sit on them for the obligatory Halloween picture. These looked nothing like those.

"You're never going to let this go, are you?" I asked, dreading her answer.

"Of course not," she laughed.

People here were different. Their hands were calloused, and their faces weathered, but they still smiled. People here found satisfaction in hard work and being productive. It was a place where you weren't judged by the brand of your clothes or what car you drove. You were judged on your character and how hard you could work. It was the first time I really saw the backbone of America. The people in the background nurturing our country. Everyone worked to their fullest capability, including us in the military. We earned every penny we made with sweat and frustration and courage. A pair of YSL heels that I might have bought before seemed excessive now: my entire E-1 paycheck for a pair of heels with less material than any other pair of shoes, yet somehow more expensive. It was pointless. I didn't have a place to wear them, and American-made is better anyway.

Seeing the old men in their plaid shirts still opening doors for their "missus." Seeing trucks covered in mud and people working in the fields, their backs bare and tanned like leather. It humbled me. The person I used to be in LA was no longer someone I would associate with. The military had given me the structure I needed and the platform that would help launch me into being a successful adult. That change came as a slow and steady series of realizations.

Looking back now, joining the military was one of the best decisions I've made. My childhood was more unstable than Britney Spears in the 2000s. My parents were never married and had split up when I was still a toddler. My mom had gone through relationships with people who didn't deserve her, and my father had struggled to get on a path that could lead to a positive outcome. Money wasn't a readily available resource. I spent a lot of time in between homes. My mom's house, my grandpa's house, other relatives' houses. I was pretty much on my own. I was loved, but my mom struggled to take care of me. I was always going from one place to another, so the slow-paced, simple life that Whiteman had brought me was a breath of fresh air. I finally had my own routine. And the best part of that routine? Payday. On the 1st and 15th of every month, we'd hop into a buddy's car and drive down to Kansas City. It was a few hours from base, but with us splitting the gas bill, it was worth the adventure. We were young and wild, seeking excitement. No one watching over us, no real financial responsibilities yet. We were really just kids.

Myspace had already taken its last dying breath. Facebook was my lifeline to the happenings of the civilian world. It also kept me in contact with Nick. He had already worked his way down most of my friends list, managing to hit up every woman I had met in the military. At first, it didn't really bother me. I had never really thought of Nick on any sort of romantic level. However, once he ghosted them, I always got an earful. I would then turn around and call Nick, yelling at him to stop hooking up with my friends. He always reacted the same…booming laughter. I was relieved when he settled down and started dating one of my friends from base.

As fate would have it, Nick was born in Missouri. When he would come home on leave, he would always make the drive up to Whiteman to see us. Facebook had made long-distance relationships a lot easier. I recently had started to date a Marine named Alex who was a military police officer (MP) down at Camp Pendleton. I had met him when I was home for Thanksgiving the year I joined the Air Force. He was incredibly good-looking but not the sharpest tool in the shed. The distance made it hard to keep a steady relationship, though. Not to mention, he had a lot of girls from back home that were constantly trying to blow up his Facebook. I started calling Nick for advice on a regular basis.

"I'm not overreacting, am I?" I asked him.

"No, definitely not, but I don't think you are being fair either," Nick said. He had a down-to-earth, no-bullshit way of calming me down.

"I just don't understand what is so hard about telling them to stop. It's not like he sees or talks to these girls anymore. At least I hope not." To be honest, I wasn't too sure about anything. I had lost faith in him.

"Is it that hard to say, 'I have a girlfriend. I don't think that's appropriate.' I say it all the time. Well, you know what I mean."

"I don't know, O'Neil. Everyone's different. Relationships aren't the same for everyone. It's not something with perfectly laid-out rules or guidelines. What might seem like an obvious answer to you could be something he never even thought of."

I rolled my eyes. Of course, he was right. Nick had sort of become my relationship Buddha.

"So, what do I do?"

"Why don't you just ask him to say that?"

"Doesn't that defeat the purpose?" If I had to ask him to do it, to me, that somehow translated into him not actually wanting to do it.

"You know, us guys are idiots. We can't always think of the same things women do. That's why sometimes we need more direction. We need you to tell us. It's like flying a plane, O'Neil. If you don't look at your instruments, you don't really know where you're going. You are his instruments." It was a crap cliché, but I liked it. Not that it had helped with Alex at all; he was just a shithead.

Alex was possessive and flirty at the same time—the worst mix. He was also immature, something that had become harder and harder for me to deal with. I was tired of his one-word text replies and his constant checkups on where I was and who I was with. I was annoyed just by the simple fact that I was even dating him. I was already at my limit that day. I needed to talk to Nick.

I went to leave a comment on his Facebook profile when a picture caught my eye. Nick had been tagged in a photo with a bunch of guys, not that that was unusual. Of course, like the young and on-the-verge-of-single girl I was, I decided to snoop. I clicked on the profile that had tagged his profile.

Jake Finley. I looked through all his photos and his tagged photos, like any sane girl would do. He looked like the kind of person who could fold himself around you, like a human fort. He was absolutely shredded, and his smile was surrounded by a halo of stubble. He was definitely what I considered "Hot." Not at all skinny, like any of the guys from Los Angeles. What I liked most about him, besides his James Bond vibes, is that in every picture I saw, it looked like he was having a blast. Jake seemed like someone who could make the best of any situation. I argued with myself for all of two seconds on whether or not I should add him. My conclusion: "F**k it." I clicked the "Add Friend" button. Not even twenty-four hours later, I received a message notification.

Hey.
You're Nick's friend, right?

It was Jake.

CHAPTER 3

Twitterpated

THERE IS ONLY ONE MAN in this world I've ever had trouble talking to: Jake. From the get-go, he made me nervous as hell. At that time, it was so hard to distinguish what type of nervous it was. The "Oh, God, what am I doing?" nervous, or the "butterflies in my stomach and fireworks" nervous. I don't sugarcoat anything. If it's an apple, I'll be the first one to call it an apple, and yet, for some reason, this man left me so nervous that I couldn't even gather coherent sentences and left me acting like a complete idiot. Which had never happened before.

There wasn't any beating around the bush with Jake. Within twenty-four hours of me adding him, he had done his research. Knowledge is power. He had already heard stories from Nick about Alex and me. In fact, I think it made him even more interested and didn't stop us from talking every night.

It was Christmas. I was supposed to be meeting up with Alex for dinner. My heart had been wavering. I hated defeat. I didn't want to give up on Alex. I wanted to use tonight as a chance for a clean slate with him. I felt giddy getting ready. It felt like I hadn't seen him in ages, which, to be honest, I hadn't. He was always busy with something, or I didn't have time. It's a strange feeling to be surrounded by people yet still feel alone. I'd almost rather be by myself. I put on a sleek black dress and curled my hair into a ponytail. Alex told me he would pick me up at seven. I looked at the clock. *6:15 PM.* I still had another forty-five minutes. I tried to keep myself busy, looking through my Facebook newsfeed, touching up my makeup, flipping through magazines, cleaning my room, refolding all my clothes, staring out the window. *7:45 PM.* I sent him a message, and then another one, and then I cleaned my room again. *8:30 PM.* This time, I called him.

"Hello?" he answered, as if he wasn't dying in a car accident like I had thought.

"Umm, where are you?" I asked. I just couldn't accept the fact that he wasn't dying from a meteor hitting his car on the way to pick me up.

"What do you mean? No need to be nosey. God, O'Neil. What's your deal?"

"What's my deal?" My top had blown off. I was already past the point of no return, and I had used the last of my patience with him weeks ago. "My deal is you, Alex! You promised me today at seven. It's Christmas, for Christ's sake! How is it that all you can fill your head with is yourself?"

"Oh, right. I forgot."

I hung up. I was furious. I looked at myself in the mirror. Such a waste. I didn't want this night to be totally ruined. So, I opened up a chat with Jake.

> *Hey.*
> *Hey. What's up? Thought you were going on some date?*
> *Things came up.*
> *Seriously? Your boyfriend's a douche. You can do so much better. Why don't you dump him and find someone who treats you better?*

I knew he was right, and I knew I had to break up with Alex. He was right. Alex was a shitty person. I closed my laptop and tried to clear my mind. I didn't want to be influenced by anyone's opinion or by feelings an internet crush gave me. But the more I thought about it, the more I felt he was right. I did deserve better. I pulled out my phone and searched for Alex. I stared at the send button for at least twenty minutes. It doesn't matter what type of relationship you're in or who does what. It sucks, especially admitting defeat, but it wasn't healthy and although we had some good memories together, it wasn't worth dealing with the constant drama. I took a deep breath and hit send.

> *We're over.*

The next day, I woke up feeling quite proud of myself and to about twenty missed calls from Alex. I checked my phone, knowing I would never return those calls, took a deep breath, and stretched out my arms and legs until my toes and fingers wiggled a sigh of sheer happiness. I couldn't help but feel relieved. I was single. No more reporting to someone details of conversations, no more getting ready for people who won't show up, no more forgotten dates. I was a free woman, and Jake had no shame in showing how happy he was about it. I had been talking to Jake daily over Skype. It was the highlight of my days. He knew just the right things to say to make me forget about Alex completely. He was like a big ball of goofy sunshine. I was talking to Jake when I heard a soft knock at my door.

"O'Neil," Emily called from behind the door. "You okay? You've been in there for a while now."

"I'm fine," I yelled.

"Is it because of Alex?"

Oh, Emily, as they like to say in the South, "bless her heart." I knew she was trying to be a good friend, but at the moment, it was so not needed. I bit my lip, looked at my computer screen, and whispered to Jake, "I'll be right back." I darted towards the door. "Emily," I said as I opened the door. I smiled. I wanted her to understand the full extent of my fineness. "I am okay. I promise."

She peered around my shoulder. Her eyes widened when her eyes met my computer screen. "Oh, okay then. I'll, um, let you go."

"Thank you," I said, grateful I didn't have to explain any more. I closed the door and ran back to my computer. "Sorry about that Jake," I said. "Emily was checking on me."

Jake smiled and waved it off. "Just wait till you meet my friends."

We talked every night this way for a year before we actually met. Jake and I would Skype for hours. His teammates would come into his dorm room occasionally and tease him.

I think they were just curious to see who he was talking to because he'd stopped hitting on girls when they would go out. Sometimes, they would try to get on Skype to talk to me, and Jake would get annoyed and close his laptop, protecting the princess from the wild beasts, as he would joke.

We weren't together, though. In fact, we had both been seeing other people on and off. We had decided that he was just too far away and that we were both too focused on our military careers to start up a serious relationship. At that time, I was busy with trying to go to college. A serious relationship didn't seem like a necessity at that time to either of us.

Combat Control Tech School (aka the "Pipeline"), the training Jake went through, is about two years long, not including the training they receive once they get to their first duty station. For the entire two years, the candidates in the Pipeline are completely pushed to their limits both mentally and physically. If they make it to Combat Control School (CCS), they earn their red beret, but just because they have a beret, it doesn't mean they're automatically an operational combat controller. They still have to do military free-fall school and pre-scuba/dive school once they graduate from CCS. Many guys will end their pursuit of becoming a combat controller, either because they are medically discharged, they wash out, or they straight up give up at this point in training. This upgraded training takes place at the Special Tactics Training School (STTS), located in a quiet little beach town in Florida.

It took me a while to figure out all these schools and the various acronyms that Jake talked about, but eventually, I caught on. These schools and their training were not designed for just anyone. It is designed to try to break you, to make you want to quit. "Never F**king Quit" is a common slogan used among the guys and in training. Of the ones that do quit, a majority are cast off because they are seen as weak. "Only the strong survive" is a very real mindset in this career choice. Just a select few make it through. To date, in the entire Department of Defense and US military, there are only around 500 combat controllers, and Jake was one of them.

As time went on, Nick ended up dating another friend of mine, Amanda, who I had met in basic training and was stationed at McGuire Air Force Base in New Jersey.

"Come on, O'Neil. Everyone needs a vacation," Nick said. He was on speakerphone with Jake.

"I don't know.... I was saving my leave to go back home," I said. It had been a long time since I had been home. My baby sister and brother were no longer babies.

"Just think about the white sandy beaches and piña coladas."

It was tempting, especially being stationed in Missouri. "I'll think about it."

Later, they started sending photos of the ocean. That slowly progressed into shirtless men on the beach, and when they got really desperate, it turned into them shirtless, holding their friend's new puppy on the beach.

I was convinced, although just the promise of an exciting time would have been enough. With me being stuck in the middle of nowhere, USA, and Amanda stuck in New Jersey, it seemed like more than enough reason to go on an adventure. We talked it over and put in a leave request for two weeks later.

The excitement hit me when my leave request came back approved. I couldn't wait to see Nick. I couldn't wait to meet the guy I'd been talking to every day on Skype. I packed up my car and drove the sixteen-hour trip straight through from Missouri to Florida. When I made it to Mississippi, it was the first time in a year that I could smell saltwater. I rolled down all my windows and breathed it in. My inner California was screaming with familiarity, and all I could think about was submerging myself in the emerald green water I had seen so many photos of. I loved the contrast the ocean brought. On the outside, a cacophony of noises: people, seagulls, waves crashing, wind howling. But, underneath, all that sound disappeared, and it was just you and the ocean.

When I finally hit the one-hour-out mark, I decided to call Nick. "Hey," I said, balancing the phone between my ear and my shoulder. "I'm an hour away."

"Awesome. I'll send you the address to this great Irish pub," he said. "You'll love it."

"I'm kind of tired. Missouri to Florida is not as easy as it sounds."

"Come on, O'Neil. It will feel good to relax and throw a cold one back. Besides, I haven't seen you in forever."

I smiled. He had me there. "Okay." After I hung up, my phone vibrated with a message. The address to the pub flashed across my screen. Guess I was headed to the beach.

I thought it would be okay to leave my hair in a mess on top of my head. I thought it would be fine if I wasn't wearing makeup. I thought it wouldn't matter if I was in a baggy sweatshirt and yoga pants. I have just been cooped up in a car for sixteen hours, and it was just Nick. Or so I thought. He was always the practical joker.

"O'Neil," he laughed. "Don't you look classy?"

"Ha-ha. I'm so amused," I said. I was amused, until I saw who was standing behind Nick. The man I had been staring at through a computer screen every day for a year looked me up and down. It was at that moment I wanted to shrink into a peanut and die. *Get yourself together*, I told myself. *They call it a "hot mess" for a reason.* I tried to play it cool and sound nonchalant. "Oh. Hey, Jake."

We sat down at a booth away from the main crowd. I stared at my hands in my lap, trying to think about all the mistakes that had let me to this point. I tried not to notice the gleaming Adonis who sat in front of me. I felt that if I let my gaze reach him, my eyes might never leave his face.

"Why are you being so weird?" Nick said.

"I'm not being weird," I said. I glared at him until it felt like my eyeballs might pop out of my head. He was not helping.

"You're totally being weird," he laughed, taking a swig of his beer.

Thankfully, the food came, so I had something else to focus on. I checked out of my peripherals to see Jake smiling warmly down at me. I couldn't tell if he was pitying me because he knew Nick ambushed me, or if he was amused at how absolutely dumbfounded I was by him. Dinner went on for what seemed like a million hours, but finally, I was able to make a quick getaway and check in to my hotel. It wasn't until the next day that I was able to meet my friend. She had met up with Nick after dinner and was preoccupied.

While Nick and Jake were at work, Amanda and I decided to have a girl's day on the beach. One of the best things about beaches on the Panhandle is, compared to Santa Monica or Miami, you can actually drink. There is nothing better than piña coladas with your girl, soaking up the sun to the sound of the ocean waves lapping the shore. I closed my eyes and breathed in the familiar smells. I was horrified that in two weeks, I would have to leave this place. To leave Jake. Missouri seemed like a black hole compared to this paradise.

As soon as the clock hit three o'clock, both of our phones rang. It was the boys. They were off work and ready to party. We thought it would be a simple dinner date, just the four of us, but let me tell you, these guys roll in packs.

Sure as shit, after dinner came drinks. Before we knew it, we were out with the boys and now, their entire team. We hit up The Swamp, a club on the island, where you could drink all you wanted for twenty dollars. So, we did. After a few drinks, the mood was high. I was sitting with Jake, who had a protective arm around me.

"So, O'Neil," he turned a sultry gaze on me.

I couldn't help but gulp. Like in the cartoons. "Yes?" I tried to sound like I wasn't melting on the inside.

"How long are you going to keep me waiting?"

"What do you mean?" My heart was doing body slams in my chest.

"Will you be my girlfriend?"

My heart fainted, and I forgot to breathe for about five seconds. Is this how cardiac arrest feels? *Hurry up, stupid. Say yes.* At least my brain was still working, but all I could manage was a timid nod. I turned my head to Amanda. She winked at me. I managed a goofy smile. To be honest, it was hard enough to contain the internal squealing, let alone maintain facial composure.

The rest of the week went by mostly the same: beach, coffee, shopping, dinner, and drinks. I pampered myself a little more than usual. It was a vacation after all. After a week of all this and being able to see Jake every day, I was in heaven.

We were going to dinner, just the two of us. I took my time getting ready. I wondered what Jake would say if he knew I skipped out on the beach with Amanda just so I could use the whole day to get ready. Maybe it was because I wanted to make up for the first day with the yoga pants. Or maybe it was because it was our first dinner date alone. Or maybe it was because I was now his girlfriend. I smiled. It still felt a little unnatural, even in my head. I gave myself one final look over. I had spent the last few hours curling my hair and making sure that my eyeliner was perfectly symmetrical. I heard a car pull up outside. I went to the window to sneak a peek. Jake leapt out of his car and bounded to my door. He had a smile reaching from one ear to another. As he stood at the door, he took a deep breath, and the smile disappeared. Instead, he replaced it with a debonair kind of smirk and a raised brow. I giggled to myself. At least I wasn't alone.

That night, he told me he loved me. I wasn't thinking that the relationship was going too fast. I was thinking that I was in paradise with the man of my dreams. My life couldn't get any better.

Jake and I, for the entire year prior, never really articulated our feelings. We always had a mutual understanding of one another in that sense. I was a lot quieter then, more of the observing type. After the men in my life had all given me the runaround, I was more guarded. But in that moment, with him staring so intensely at me, I knew, we were both absolutely twitterpated. Just like the scene in *Bambi*.

My two-week vacation was over in the blink of an eye. A summer storm made the day I was leaving even more dramatic.

Jake had to be at training at 4:30 in the morning, so we said our goodbyes the hour before. I could tell by the look in his eyes he wanted me to stay permanently.

"I'll come see you as often as I can," Jake said. I rolled my eyes, I figured that would mean once every couple of months. "I promise," he said. He kissed me first on the forehead, and then his warm lips found mine. It was an intense kiss, with so many emotions—love, sadness, hope, promise. His breath was heavy and sweet and stuck with me even as I started the sixteen-hour drive home. As the grey clouds waved goodbye and the rain whispered melancholy goodbyes, I couldn't help but know that where I just was, was my new home.

Jake wasn't lying when he told me he would see me as often as he could. He flew out to see me every other weekend. And I had only been back in Missouri a month before he coolly suggested we get married. To say I was startled was an understatement. For one, for as much as we struggled, my mother eventually put herself through college and law school and became a divorce attorney who worked for a pretty well-known law firm. She told me horror stories on a regular basis. Now that I think about it, I wonder if it was her way of instilling caution in me.

I was also only twenty. I had just joined the military, and I had promised myself that I would be strong and independent, that I wasn't ready for a serious relationship and I wanted to focus on school. Of course, I had no way of predicting the connection I would make with Jake. So, there I was, considering marriage, which scared the crap out of me. I didn't exactly have the picturesque image growing up of healthy relationships modeled before me.

I thought about it a little more. Missouri was terrible. I hated it. Jake was everything I thought was epic. I was young, and it was the prime time for split-second decisions. So, I said yes. He put in leave for Veterans Day weekend and again flew out to Missouri. I made the two-hour drive to pick him up from the airport, and we began our Craigslist journey to find a justice of the peace to do the deed on a federal holiday.

We didn't quite win in the Craigslist department, but the internet never fails. We ended up finding a guy to marry us for sixty bucks at a small coffee shop near base. I nearly fainted from relief after we signed the paperwork and had mutually decided that we were not going to tell our parents we got married. I could just imagine my mom's reaction; it wouldn't have been pretty. But all's well that ends well. I couldn't even legally drink, so after the paperwork was finished, we celebrated by going into Kansas City for dinner at The Cheesecake Factory.

That Monday, I came into work and told everyone I had gotten married. I've never been a very public person with my relationship status, so they were surprised and, in some cases, pissed. A lot of them thought I was single and not dating anyone. I worked with a ton of pilots, so eventually, everyone in my shop and all the flying squadrons found out that I had gotten married. Needless to say, hearts were broken.

They all wanted to know who Jake was and what he did. So, I told them. I still had no idea myself what he did, but when I told them, I could see their reactions change and immediate respect surfaced for a man that they had never met. Although, it didn't stop them from publicly calling me out at Commander's Call for getting married to my boyfriend of a month. Nor did it stop them from giving me a hard time for my impending departure.

I was given official orders to change duty stations exactly one month after we tied the knot. I drove away from that base and never looked back. I knew at that point in my life that I was on a new adventure. For the first time in my life, I had no idea what was going to happen next, and I couldn't have been more excited.

CHAPTER 4

Florida

For the second time in a year, I made the sixteen-hour trip down to my favorite place and new home. I wanted to surprise Jake, so I told him I would be leaving the following day. The military allots a certain amount of driving time per day when changing duty stations. He wasn't expecting me for a few days because I was allotted this time to make the trip.

Thankfully, he was doing training that day, so it was a bit easier to be sneaky. He did, however, manage to call me about four times to check in. Little did he know, I was already well on my way to see him.

"What are you doing?" he asked.

"Just driving to get some dinner in Knob Noster," I said.

"How come every time I call you, you're in the car?"

I laughed. "Good timing? How's training?"

"It's training. I can't wait to get home and pass out."

"I feel you," I said.

"What do you have to be tired about?"

Shit. Almost blew my cover. "I have just been out and about all day, plus trying to prepare for the move and everything. I'm just exhausted."

"Well, hurry and go eat. That way you can go back to rest."

"I will."

I hung up the phone and turned my music back on. I was passing through Jasper, Alabama. It was just another small southern town. Full of pickups and colonial-style homes, sprinkled with Confederate flags and statues of old fallen heroes. After being in Missouri for some time and assimilating into the country lifestyle, I realized that these flags were not flown as a symbol of racism; it was simply part of the heritage of the South. Now, back in my LA days, I would have never understood that, but after about two years of being in the military and outside the LA bubble, I started realizing a lot.

I thought about all the places I had been and where I was going. Never in a million years did I think I would be a "Mrs." this soon, yet here I was, driving to see someone who set my heart on fire. I was his. I felt like I couldn't contain the emotions going through my body. I was excited to start my new life.

I worried about the fact that I was legally married to the man who finally understood me but that I didn't quite feel like I even really knew him yet. It's like when you order something expensive from a restaurant. You treasure each bite, and you're happy about how good it tastes, but in the back of your mind, you are worried about whether it's really worth how expensive it is. Even so, it is too late, and you just try to enjoy the moment and not think about anything else but how it's melting in your mouth. You pretend you aren't letting your mind wander to the price and to your bills and to how you promised yourself you would budget this month but are instead spending money frivolously and should really stop buying Starbucks. Before you know it, you've scarfed the whole thing down and missed out on savoring the flavors. But at the same time, you have this content, full feeling, so you smile anyways.

I let my thoughts wander as the yellow lines in the road blurred together. I arrived at Jake's house about an hour after he sent me his goodnight text message. I never replied hoping he would think I had already fallen asleep. I pulled into the driveway and sat in the car with the lights off—partly because I wanted to make sure he was asleep and partly because I was trying to calm myself. I had just turned twenty-one. The only man I had ever somewhat lived with before this was my dad. But here I was, secretly married, about to secretly start living together. It felt a little childish, but I still thought things would be better this way.

It took me calling twice to get an answer. But when he finally picked up, he about jumped through the phone when I told him I was outside, waiting for him to let me in. He hung up immediately, flew down the stairs, and gave me the longest, biggest bear hug I'd yet to experience in my life.

It's funny how you adjust to the people around you based on the amount of love you have for that person. When you really love someone, you can do anything to make things work. If it's an acquaintance or friend, you have a line that you draw at certain points. If it's family, that line is movable, depending on different situations. Jake taught me that giving up wasn't always a bad thing if it meant we could be happy—especially when it came to little things like the toothpaste cap and which way the toilet paper roll went. I learned that living with someone isn't easy, no matter how much you love them, and if you can't compromise, then you might as well call it quits. One person can't be making all the sacrifices. One person can't carry all of the burden. One person can't be the glue to hold a relationship together. It takes two to tango, baby. I think that is one thing I will always be grateful to Jake for. Adjusting to Jake was hard at first, but like everything else in life, it got easier with time.

Adjusting to my new job on base, however, was quite a walk in the park. I had gone from twelve-hour shifts and no holidays off to eight-hour shifts and no more than forty hours a week. At Whiteman, it had been 365 days a year, rain or shine, with no such things as holidays. Now, I felt like I had a normal life. Not to mention the aircraft were low maintenance, and the leadership was way less dramatic. Wish I could say the same of most of the women in the military. You'd think we would try to stick together, being a minority. Unfortunately, that is not the case.

Jealousy can get the better of anyone, especially of women in the military. If you have a supervisor who's a woman, or a woman who outranks you in your section or command, you pray to God she's normal. I tried to stay optimistic, but I was usually proven wrong, and so were my friends. I've seen a large percentage use their authority to try to get other women in trouble under the guise of "guidance." I had been lucky to have mostly men as supervisors at the last few duty assignments, so when women tried to punk me, my superiors always saw right through it and had my back. I also became well versed and very good at looking up regulations in order to defend myself.

Of all the articles that exist in the media about harassment of women in the military, it's rare that you see one about women harassing other women. But in my experience, I received far more vicious harassment from women. It is especially bad if you are pretty. There is no end to the excuses people start to make for your success. They try to turn every accomplishment into something to be ashamed about or something you were given. And they always refuse to acknowledge that you may have genuinely earned it on merit.

With the rise of social media, it only got worse. I feel bad for any decent-looking military woman because I know for a fact that they will be confronted with this treatment at some point in their careers. Regardless of looks or gender or race, trying to demean someone's achievements because you feel you haven't had the same opportunities is wrong. Look really long and hard at yourself first and ask yourself if you've really done everything in your power to change what you can. Then ask yourself if you honestly know the other person well enough to make inferences about what they have gone through and the challenges they've had to face. One of the biggest flaws of our generation is our lack of ability to be honest with ourselves. We make excuses to feel better about ourselves and our situations instead of actually putting in the work to change anything.

For as much as I tried, women in the military that I could actually trust and connect with were few and far between. That is why I was thankful when I finally met Ace.

Ace was a dental hygienist on base. People quickly noticed us together both on and off base for a few reasons. One, we were always together, and two, we looked like we could be sisters. I hadn't had a best friend like this that was actually in the military since I joined, and after I met her, we quickly became inseparable. Not only was she like a sister to me, but she was also dating another controller. It was nice to have someone to vent to who really understood, and believe me, there were always things to vent about.

I quickly adjusted to doing things on my own. Jake was still in training and was gone for a total of 300 days during my first year in Florida. The time away from home was actually such a problem that eventually, the Air Force issued guidance via their Air Force Instruction (AFI) for leadership that outlined the maximum amount of time men were to be away from their families during their training cycles. This was the time in the career field when leadership became concerned about the home life of men in the military. The divorce rate at this time in the combat control career field was upward of 90 percent, and there was a reason for that.

Jake and I lived in a modest townhome one block away from the beach and less than a mile from base. My daily routine was work, gym, beach, and school—not a bad assignment for the US military. There was only one tiny little downside to where we were stationed, and that was the partying element. Where our base was located also happened to be the spring break capital of the world. We had people flying in from all over the United States, especially the South, during spring break and in the summertime.

There was definitely no shortage of beach bars. The first summer I moved down there, I discovered, courtesy of Jake and his team, that you could drink all you wanted to at three different bars for a total of twenty dollars. This probably gave the base commander a headache, as there was never a shortage of DUIs on the weekends. Lucky for us, I had myself volunteered for Airmen Against Drunk Driving (AADD) when I was at Whiteman and had no problem calling the number listed on the base light board when I needed a ride home. Once the other guys also discovered they could do this, we became frequents on the AADD hotline.

Florida was a smooth transition. It was sunny, I could go to the beach whenever I wanted, and I had Jake living with me. It was also at Hurlburt that my supervisor said they would work with my schedule and allow me to take courses at the local college. I was now twenty-one and working full-time for the military. I was newly, secretly married and also going to school. Everything was perfect, but as they say, all good things come to an end.

CHAPTER 5

The Guys

IMAGINE THE PLAYBOY LIFESTYLE OF Batman, the cunningness of a fox, the body and capability of a professional athlete, and a dash of cockiness. Voilà, I give you any freshly graduated combat controller or their counterpart, a pararescueman (PJ for short). Even the military puts them on a pedestal, and rightfully so. They are the best of the best. I would even go as far as saying that this personality type was the same across every branch of the military, including the Seals and Green Berets.

Rules don't run the same for these guys as they do in the conventional side of the house, nor should they. From the time they join, they know only a small percentage of them will make it through. They are continuously tested and evaluated through every step of the process. All the instructors know the long journey that each of these men will endure. They know what it takes and what they need to have to stay alive when they deploy. If they see any bit of weakness in their character or in them, they are eliminated from the program. The ones that make it through have done so on sheer will. They refuse to quit.

When the guys are in their pipeline, they are separated into teams. The teams do everything together, literally—whether it is training trips, holidays, deployments, funerals, weddings, or, in some cases, women. They develop a bond that they carry with them into their operational military careers once they are officially deemed controllers and have left the schoolhouse.

When out, you can always tell who is at the schoolhouse versus who has actually deployed. The schoolhouse controllers and/or PJs are like young puppies. They are always loud and wild and give off the vibe that they are at the top of the world. It saddens me to actually say it, but it is at this point that I genuinely feel that they are the happiest in their entire careers. They are just about to head off to their operational units. They have their best friends, are full of life, and are getting laid every weekend.

They're typically in their early twenties, have just started working on their sleeves, and all wear the same clothing. It's funny seeing them out and trying to blend in. Their outfits are always a dead giveaway.

Rule of thumb goes: if you see a group of about five to seven guys wearing flannels, Suunto watches, Salomon shoes, baseball caps with Velcro, and a half-finished sleeve of tattoos on one arm, I'd bet 99 percent of the time it's a team of young controllers, PJs, or both. The younger, newer guys will always roll out together, and when they roll, they roll deep.

The guys who have seen two or three deployments typically roll solo to the bars when it comes to meeting friends.

They can pull any chick and are usually grumpy as f**k. Imagine an old walrus, scarred and dominating. They sit away from the crowds, and for some reason, the quiet 'I'm going to kick your ass vibe' only intrigues women even more. It isn't until the new guys get to their units that they are very quickly put in their places. Many times, depending on the team they are assigned to, they will have to do certain things until another new guy comes along.

It's better than joining a fraternity. It's acceptance into an elite group of men—the type of men that Hollywood writes about in screenplays, that men pretend to be in video games, and that our history books record. Most of the new guys are very aware of this fact and very quickly know that they must prove themselves if they want to stay a part of the team, and every team, no matter what unit or duty station, has its own unique theme.

At the Special Tactics Squadron (STS) Jake was assigned to, for example, each team had a way of indoctrinating their new guys. The new guy on Jake's team would have to carry a massive hammer. It was made from a concrete cinder block and painted gold to represent the hammer of Thor. It was actually done pretty well, and at a first glance, you would never think it was anything more than décor for their team room. Jake's team symbol was a Berserker, a fierce warrior fighter in Norse mythology who, in a fury of rage, would open up on the battlefield and slaughter anything in its path.

Carrying these items and the indoctrination into a team is not hazing. It's done to remind the new guys of their place in the pecking order. It is done to remind them that just because they had graduated at the schoolhouse, they had not yet seen war. If they wanted to be respected by their team, they'd have to earn their place among the men. Even at the team levels, if you show that you cannot do your job or cannot make the cut psychologically, you are simply kicked off the team. Following orders and being able to trust in the team, is the difference between life and death on the battlefield.

Occasionally, Jake would come home with a story of one of the new guys, whether it was on his team or another, who suffered from ego issues. Those guys never stayed that way for long. In this career field, they don't give you paperwork. If you piss someone off, they physically break you. It wasn't uncommon for me to show up at the unit and observe someone doing "towers." This was a common punishment where the individual had to run sandbags up nine flights of stairs and build a defensive fighting position only to bring it all back down again, one sandbag at a time, when they were done.

In the military, it's also pretty safe to say that drinking is socially acceptable. It's more of a bonding situation than anything. There is definitely a certain level of comradery that is brought on by going out and having a few beers with your coworkers. We drink to celebrate, we drink for fun, and we drink to mourn.

Regardless of what any health survey will say, like the annoying annual survey that the military health clinics will send out, or what any public affairs representative for the military tell you, politically correct or not, drinking and the military go hand in hand. It's part of the lifestyle.

Now, if this is something that is commonly accepted in conventional military, imagine the amount of drinking and bonding that goes down with someone in special tactics. For most of their careers, these dudes are completely at their peak regarding physical fitness. I can attest to the fact that there were a few times during Jake's pipeline when he and his team would drink beer in order to carb-load for their AFSOC fitness test. I don't care how much you pride yourself in drinking—they will very quickly drink you under the table. I learned that the hard way trying to keep up.

At some of the team parties, guys new to the team, guys leaving the military, or guys moving to a different duty station had to "yard-in" and "yard-out." They would drink one yard of beer for a recorded time to attempt to break the fastest record. It was always hilarious to watch because if they did it in a decent time, they were punished with more beer, but if their lips left the cup at any point during the contest, they would have to restart.

This meant, even if they threw up in their glass, they had to continue drinking or they faced having to restart the yard. Time wasn't taken until the yard was fully empty and they could hold the glass empty over their head. In Jake's case, when it came time for him to leave his team, they had their own rendition of the yard that was called "Carling-in" and "Carling-out." This referred to the Carl Gustaf shell that they had been converted into a beer stein by their original team sergeant who, while in Afghanistan, killed a Taliban member with a Carl Gustaf that had almost shot and killed him. In memory of his near-death experience, he made a mug out of the winning shell that all the guys would essentially pay tribute to during their coming or going.

Our house quickly became the gathering place for everyone when we would go out. Every Friday and Saturday night, Ace and a few of my girlfriends would come over, and Jake would rally his teammates. The bars were open until 4 AM, so we never headed out until 11 PM. We would kill time at our place pre-gaming and playing various drinking games. This was the summer of Four Lokos, and I'm pretty sure that that drink was responsible for at least three spontaneous pregnancies at Jake's STS, followed by a shotgun wedding and divorce.

Although I did not live on my college campus, I didn't think I was missing much. I had gone to a few fraternity parties in high school, and hanging out with this group of guys was no different. The only thing I ever noticed that ever got between them was a woman, and that was a pretty rare occurrence.

There was one girl that I met a few times in passing who was very cute. She had been dating one of the guys for a little over a year, and right before he got orders to his permanent duty station, he broke up with her. I could tell she was devastated, but it quickly turned into a spite campaign; each night, she was seen leaving a different room. I was pretty horrified when I heard her nicknamed "dorm-rat." Her ex found out and wasn't even mad. He, in fact, was more disgusted than anything, and he was later heard telling his buddies about how it helped him "get over" the entire relationship.

If there is one thing these guys never do, it is hold grudges. They don't feel the need to compete, as they come equipped with reinforced egos that are almost impossible to break. Where there is a loss of one girl, typically, they are quickly replaced, and it is seldom a downgrade.

CHAPTER 6

The Groupies

It wasn't until my first duty assignment in Missouri that I realized that the concept of a "military groupie" was an actual thing. One of my friends, who was an explosive ordnance disposal technician, called me one night and asked me to show up to dinner at a local restaurant with him. He had taken this bartender, who happened to work there, out on a few dates, only to find out that she had slept with four of his coworkers.

He wanted to make her jealous and used the oldest trick in the book: calling another pretty girl to dangle in front of his ex. He was one of my best friends at Whiteman, so I willingly accepted his invitation. Of course, she hated me instantly, and I never got good service at that restaurant again. But that night, I got free dinner, and he got his revenge. He made her jealous. It was after that night that I became aware that this type of woman was not a rarity. I was aware that there were groupies for professional athletes, bands, and artists—but military groupies? That had to take the cake.

It never really bothered me because I figured you should be able to date who you want, but when I started realizing that my friends were being targeted as prospects because of their jobs or the fact that they were in the military? It weirded me out. Yes, there are even women in the military who ONLY date controllers. Maybe it's an ego thing, being able to date the typical alpha male, but I'd be willing to bet it's a money thing more often than not.

During Jake's training in Mississippi, even his instructors warned him about the SOF (Special Operation Forces) groupies within the military. Before every weekend brief, they would warn them to stay away from the "triangle" girls. The triangle was the nickname for the dormitories where the tech school trainees stayed that surrounded the courtyard at Keesler Air Force Base. It was common, especially in tech school, for the guys going through training to run into these girls at the chow halls. Having been stationed there myself, I saw this firsthand on a regular basis.

At least around the base in Florida, the guys usually had better luck, and the locals weren't that bad. However, we always had our guard up. Once we found out one of the guys was dating a groupie, we all had pretty solid predictions about how their relationship would end, and we were usually right. You just knew that about 90 percent of the time, they would end up divorced somewhere down the line, or they would end up a wife who refused to work, only to consistently plug into the gossip network and pop out kids, and that the guys would end up cheating on them.

If they were groupies, they looked at them like they were walking, talking baby donors with a guaranteed 401(k) and made no effort in hiding that fact. Children are usually their guaranteed financial plan B, just in case things don't work out. The more I started going out with Jake and the guys, the more I started to pick up on this type of person. Eventually, I myself had to become very selective about who I chose to associate with.

It's easy to spot. The neon signs on their foreheads especially light up when they are at someone's house party. You'll hear a civilian woman rattle off every CCT acronym, talk about deployments, how all her "friends" are in the military, and, in some shameless instances, about the financial bonus given to those of us who decide to re-enlist. For Jake's job, that was usually an extra $80,000 or more and somehow, the groupies found that out.

"Beret Chaser." "Cone Slayer." "Tricare-itops." "Dependasaurus." These are all actual terms (usually not the nicest) used by the guys and other service members to describe the various classes of military groupies. Beret Chasers will only date and marry a PJ. If you aren't a PJ, they won't even look at you. The Cone Slayer is a bit more descriptive, referencing the nickname given to the enlisted, non-operational controller student who is still going through the training pipeline. This is a term used for the groupie that sticks to hooking up with the student controllers. In Florida, however, because the schoolhouse and the operational unit are on the same base, sometimes these women will go back and forth between operational and schoolhouse controllers. The Tricare-itops and Dependasaurus are similar species. Unlike loving and devoted stay-at-home moms, they do nothing but stay at home, spit out kids, and gossip—all in an effort to cement and snare their service members into a lifelong obligation of support and "marriage."

It's not uncommon to hear of groupies sleeping around or hooking up with multiple guys on a team or teams. It doesn't matter if they are married or not. Most of the groupies are about four or more PJs deep before they end up somewhat locking one down. What they don't know, though, is that all guys talk. If you think a woman is the only one to gossip, you are wrong. They know exactly who is dating who and they don't hold back with the details.

I cannot tell you how many of these women entrap a guy by either forcing a marriage before the guy would get sent to his final duty station or lying about being on birth control and getting pregnant whether they are dating (or not). It seems self-explanatory to say this type of relationship never lasts. The poor guy will marry the groupie in an attempt to correct the problem after finding out she is pregnant. They will do the shotgun wedding, stay married for a few years, maybe have another child, maybe two deployments at most, and then divorce. For some reason, women think you can keep a man by getting pregnant, but the fact of the matter is if he's not interested, neither you nor a baby will keep him. You cannot entrap a Type A man with pregnancy and the only person that truly ends up suffering is the child.

These women are the type that have no self-worth. They think the only way they can keep a man is by having a baby. They are lazy. Instead of focusing on building a real and lasting relationship, they focus on ways to trick and trap. Like a black widow, waiting to devour the next male that crosses her path, they sit at the local bars frequented by military personnel and wait to sink their fangs in the next one.

There was one case of groupie-ism that sent Jake's entire unit into a downward spiral. Sam was a PJ who had started dating one of the better-known groupies. To his credit, I think he really thought he could change her, or was hoping to anyways. They had dated for quite a while, but her level of crazy even started to concern some of the guys, and initially, he would make excuses, until he realized that it was very possible that she was a compulsive liar and obsessively jealous to boot. While he was deployed, he received screenshots from one of his teammates of her trying to hang out with him on Facebook. He even caught her sending nudes to old guys that would come into her work for money. She had been a waitress in town.

The problem was that Sam was deployed. This type of emotional rollercoaster really could get someone killed. Especially in their line of work. Distracted is something you NEVER want to be, especially deployed, and everyone knew it. So before he got back, there was almost a collective decision among the guys to ice her out. No one would talk to her anymore or return her calls and as soon as Sam got back, he kicked her out of his house, but not before she tore it apart in a fit of rejection.

Sam later on sat down with a few of us and vented. There was no question that she was unstable, but I realized that Sam was really hurting regardless of the front he put on. The girl he had been planning to marry had betrayed him. He went around for weeks apologizing to anyone and everyone at the unit that she had caused problems with. Initially his head hung low, he was embarrassed, and but eventually, he became relieved. He probably forgot why he was even apologizing in the first place. I think we all did. Recovery from that type of emotional abuse and manipulation is a steep and rocky road, but dodging that bullet is something every guy eventually is glad for. The moral of this story is: stop making excuses for someone when they continuously take you for granted. Sam was a good guy and deserved more than that.

I learned a few things early on with the guys, with a little help from Jake's insight:

1. I couldn't just tell any chick, especially if she was local and trying to be my friend, that I was married to a controller.
2. I couldn't bring friends that I wanted to continue a friendship with around the guys, especially Jonas, Jake's best friend and teammate.
3. Hurlburt Field is very publicly recognized as the headquarters of the Air Force Special Operations Command. Between the military chicks on base and the local groupies, as crude as it may sound, never have so many women actively pursued a group of guys until I met this bunch.

I started realizing that I had to be careful when random women would approach me while I was out and introduce themselves. The conversations generally started the same. They had seen me on my buddy's Facebook. Then, after they first established communication, they would comment here and there on social media and eventually start texting me when they knew I was going out with the guys.

Like clockwork, they would always hook up with one or a few of the guys on the first night they met, and then couldn't comprehend why they wouldn't get a call back. Then, eventually at some point, when they would see our buddies out with another girl, my phone would blow up with countless angry texts. It became a headache.

In the case of Jonas, who happened to be Jake's best friend and teammate, I'm pretty convinced it was a game to him to see how many of my friends he could sleep with. Not one of my friends managed to escape his scheming. His baby face paired with the physique of the statue of David was an instant killer. He always used the innocent card, and regardless of my fair warnings to them, they would always fall for it. When that type of temptation is in front of you, it's hard to resist. The thrill of being with the best of the best. The need to nurture their broken souls, to be the girl that changes their frivolous ways. Mix that together with being able to smooth talk Velvet into doing anything, and you had Jonas. He was a force. And by the time I had left Florida, and to my dismay, he had managed to sleep with every single one of my friends.

Of course, after his final conquest, I could never have any two friends in the same room because they all developed that awkward animosity that two women will have when they've slept with the same guy. I loved Jonas as a brother, but his male gigolo persona was a problem. I decided to never bring around a friend I anticipated on having any long-term friendship with, out of fear that Jonas would prey on her.

CHAPTER 7

The Spouses' Club

IT TOOK ME A WHILE to transition into what other STS wives would consider a married role. I didn't start making an active effort to associate with the married aspect of the community until we had already been married for about two years. Mainly because at this point, my schooling had taken over much of my free time and I was already the target of bored women's gossip. When I did finally muster up the courage to attend, the event left me feeling so guilty and traumatized, I avoided the squadron functions for a long time after that.

Jake had come home one Friday after work and mentioned that his team was having a barbeque.

"Want to go?" he asked.

"Of course," I said. I was actually excited to meet everyone. I had just moved to Florida and was on a friend hunt. "Maybe I can make some friends."

"I'm sure everyone will love you."

As soon as I walked in the door, I saw the eyes of every woman at the barbeque look me up and down. I could instantly tell I was new blood to them.

"How long have you been married?" one asked me.

"Not that long," I said.

"Mmmm," she said.

Every single one of them began to grill me, except one. They asked me questions about my position and about my relationship with Jake. And each answered with some sort of knowing "mmm," as if they thought my short answers were a tell-all to my relationship. The girl who gave me a sympathetic smile was engaged to Jake's teammate, SSgt. Hayden. All the guys were getting ready to graduate from the STTS and go to their operational units. Most of the families come out a week prior, but since she and SSgt. Hayden were in a long-distance relationship, she came out early to spend some time with him. I took to her immediately. She was also from a big city, and we clicked instantly.

"What do you miss most?" she asked me.

We had found a quiet corner and were trying to avoid the prying eyes and ears of the others. "Shopping," I said with a smile.

"Is it hard for you?" she asked.

I could tell she was being genuine. "Sometimes," I told her honestly, "I miss my family, but I am happy with where I am right now."

She looked at SSgt. Hayden, "Me too."

We ended up playing corn hole, and after a few hours, Jake and I left. I was happy that I had actually made a friend, especially since I knew I would probably see her again, being that she was dating one of the guys—that was, until right after they graduated. I saw SSgt. Hayden out at the Swamp, a local beach bar, making out with a random girl who was in town for spring break. I couldn't bear the thought of running into his fiancée.

I couldn't look this woman in the eyes and pretend to be her friend and not tell her what I had seen. Lucky for me, SSgt. Hayden ended up getting orders to a base in England, and I never ran into her again, but the entire experience still left a bad taste in my mouth.

Needless to say, that wasn't the only time this happened. About two weeks later, I hit my last nerve. Jake and I were out at dinner one night prior to attending a birthday party. On our way out of the restaurant, we ran into Aaron, a PJ in Jake's unit. He was with a very pretty girl. She was super tan and had long dark hair and clear, blue eyes. She was the kind of girl you see in beach getaway ads.

"This is my girlfriend," Aaron said, putting a protective arm around her shoulder.

She smiled from ear to ear. "Nice to meet you. I'm Samantha."

"I'm Jake, and this is my wife, O'Neil," Jake said.

I reached out my hand and shook hers. "Nice to meet you." She seemed nice enough, and her shy smile was refreshing.

"What are y'all doing tonight? Want to grab a drink?" Aaron asked.

"Sorry, we're running late to a friend's birthday," Jake said. "How about a raincheck?"

"Yeah, let's meet up later this week. Just shoot me a text, bro," Aaron said as he reached his fist out.

"You got it," Jake said smashing his own fist into Aaron's. I waved goodbye to Samantha and Aaron, and we headed off to our friends.

That following weekend, we were out with Jake's team. We headed to the usual spot, a bar called The Green Door Saloon. Right as we walked in, we spotted Aaron with an absolutely gorgeous tall brunette, tan, and blue-eyed girl. Jake and Aaron walked off to the bar. The girl was fidgeting some lint on her dress. I could see she felt nervous. There were a ton of people with us, and she was one of the few women in the group. I knew how she felt, and since I had met her the week prior, I smiled, walked over, and hugged her.

"Hey! How are you enjoying the sun? Way different than Chicago, huh?" I said.

She looked at me puzzled. "Well, hi. Um, do I know you?" she asked with a nervous smile.

"Yeah, we met last week. You were with Aaron at dinner."

"What are you talking about?" she looked confused.

I started to wonder whether the girl got amnesia sometime between when I last met her and now. "At the restaurant?" I told her. "You're from Chicago. Samantha."

Her face changed. "My name isn't Samantha."

She turned to look at Aaron furiously. I turned to look at Jake, horrified and confused. She grabbed her phone from her purse and started smashing the keys in a rapid fury. I stealthily made my getaway and headed towards Jake.

"You did what?" he asked.

"How was I supposed to know?" I whisper yelled. "They look exactly the same. It's dark."

"I have to tell Aaron."

Aaron nodded as Jake whispered in his ear. He looked at me and winked before turning to the bartender and ordering two shots. He carried the glasses to the girl and smiled. To my surprise, she smiled back and downed the shot without hesitation. There was no big explosion. No storming out. She was completely calm, which worried me even more.

They had a couple more drinks together. She took another shot and then said, "Aaron, can I talk to you?" Before he could even respond, she asked, "Do you have a girlfriend?" We couldn't make out his response, but his face said it all. Before I knew it, she screamed, "Are you f**king kidding me?" and walked out of the bar. I was more or less horrified that I had accidentally just outed one of our friends. I felt terrible and told Aaron I was sorry. He actually started laughing, and to my surprise, I realized he really didn't care.

He ended up dumping his actual girlfriend, Samantha, a few days later. After that fiasco, I realized that I would really not have anything to do with these women if it weren't for Jake. I had my own career, life, and friends, and it was less heartache to just avoid the wives and girlfriends altogether. I didn't want to be the reason for, or affiliated with, the ending of a relationship, whether they were marriages, dating, or engagements. I could never keep it straight with who was actually married, cheating, or dating. On top of that, my conscience would eat at me if I didn't say anything, and I never did have a good poker face. If you are a decent human being, it's pretty hard to sit back and pretend to be friends with someone, knowing all the while that they're being cheated on.

"Girl code" stipulates you have to let the other woman know. However, team code says literally, "don't be a buddy f**ker." This was Jake's world, not mine. So, I kept my mouth shut—not because I wanted to, but because I didn't want to cause drama for my husband at his workplace. Saying something would only cause problems for guys that are considered his friends. In their eyes, it's not my business to keep track of a moral standard of what's going on in other people's personal lives.

I was completely unaware that something called "the spouses' club" existed at Jake's squadron until about two years into our marriage. At my own unit clear across base, I had heard of what the spouses' club did. I myself had accidentally been added to the email distribution list as a "spouse" and would periodically get an update of their invitations to social luncheons and party planning functions. At my unit, the spouses' club was in charge of planning the annual Christmas party, squadron fundraisers, and holiday events, but at a special tactics squadron, based on observation alone, they're a different breed of woman and a whole different breed of spouse.

Although I have always been a very independent person, I could see where most women with no military affiliation, such as spouses, fiancées, and girlfriends, would need the support network of a spouses' club, and I thought it was actually a pretty good idea. As a whole, it can be hard to move constantly from one location to the next, be essentially a single parent because your other half is deployed or TDY, and be alone often. The spouses' clubs are intended to provide a support network to the wives.

Now, special tactics squadrons are a bit different than those of the conventional military. Truthfully, if you marry into this community, they're gone a lot. Between their deployment cycles and the training they have to do, you are on your own a majority of the time. You accept it as being part of his job, but it doesn't make it suck any less. I was lucky enough to have Ace, but most of these women had moved from other states to be with their controllers or pararescuemen, and a majority were not affiliated with the military in any way. It was because of this that the spouses' club at the special tactics squadrons are usually beefier in regard to their extracurricular events and funding versus the other conventional spouses' clubs. Mainly for this reason: Imagine the adjustment that would happen when someone's spouse would leave…not just for a few weeks, but on average, half a year. In my case, it was always a weird adjustment when Jake would leave. You go from spending as much time as you can with someone, to zero contact and limited conversation.

I'd be lying if I said I didn't take it pretty hard the first week that he would leave. There were many times where I would put on my happy face as he was walking to his terminal, only to make it about one minute into my drive back home sobbing at the fact that he was going to be gone for half the year. Granted, I never exactly wanted to admit that I had gotten this emotionally attached to anyone, but it truly was one of the hardest things I had to do. Not just once, but five times.

I compensated by burying myself in work, classes, and at the gym. I was thankful for that because it did help pass the time, but there were many nights when I couldn't sleep, so regardless of the time, I would head to the gym on base that was open twenty-four hours.

My coworkers must have loved it, because I actually made it a point while Jake was deployed to request night shifts. For me, it actually helped me feel closer to him. If I worked nights, I knew we would be on the same schedule. This meant we could talk more and when he called I would be awake to answer. Missing calls was always the worst because regardless of how much you try to coordinate, internet outages are your worst enemy.

The spouses' club at any unit, whether it is in special tactics or in a conventional military unit, is usually led by the commander's wife or the squadron chief's wife. Typically, they will hold small luncheons, dinners, and, at least at our unit, spa days. A majority of them even have their own Facebook page. Upon entry processing at any unit, the men have the ability and are asked for the email of their spouse, fiancée, or serious girlfriend.

The spouses' club is supposed to be welcoming and friendly to all, but in the controller and pararescueman community, it is hard not to notice that a majority of the wives are super cliquey and, in my opinion, for all the wrong reasons. There's also a huge difference in the personalities between the controllers' wives and the pararescuemen's wives. For some reason, across the board, there seems to be a general attraction from these men to women in the medical field. The PJs always end up getting married to nurses or dating hippies, and the controllers' wives, well, they tend to either be batshit crazy or insanely successful in their own right. There is no in-between.

As it turned out, my childhood friend, who I actually simultaneously enlisted in the Air Force with, ended up marrying an officer pararescueman. This, of course, completely changed the dynamic of when I would go to these events solo versus when she would come with me. This would make us giggle because her being an officer's wife was no different to me than any of the other enlisted spouses, but to some of these women, the brown-nosing was painfully obvious, and we both knew it. As we were talking about the spouses' club one day, we had a lightbulb moment regarding the personality types. It always was a rather entertaining subject because the stereotypes tended to be right.

Among the wives themselves, it is usually assumed that the controller wives generally drink more and are crazier and louder than the pararescuemen's wives. I can tell you, being a controller wife myself, that this is somewhat true. However, the pararescuemen's wives tend to be more laid-back in my opinion. Seeing all the "plus ones" at the spouses' events and annual Christmas parties makes for a rather entertaining event.

The more I got involved in the community, the more I started realizing something about the wives as a whole, especially the ones that "wear their husband's beret" or "wear their rank." You would swear these women went through the pipeline themselves with the egos they bring to the table.

In Ace's case, she was one of my closest friends, but she was also technically a girlfriend, not a wife or fiancée. So, to my frustration, the wives made sure she knew her place. Even when she would show up for her boyfriend's deployment homecomings, they would glare at her. She could never do anything right. Either she wasn't dressed how they liked, she didn't behave how they wanted, or she was too loud. They always had something to say about her and frankly, she wasn't the only woman I saw this happen to. I saw this happen to countless women in and out of the military, at various Special Tactics Units, some of which were support personnel who worked at the various units with the guys.

The military, as large as it is, is a very close network of people. To give you some perspective, if you are in the military, at any base you go to, you will likely meet someone who has worked with one of your coworkers from your last base or knows someone you know. Being that the special tactics community is so small, this is amplified. Both words and reputations travel fast.

In the military in general, women as a whole make up a small percentage. I wish I could tell you that military women stick together, but that's simply not the case. I liked to call it "small pond syndrome" with the way some women acted. They get inflated egos due to the amount of male attention they receive from other military members, and any other woman disrupting that, especially a coworker, is an immediate threat, and it makes them mean.

If there was one thing I became very accustomed to while I was in the military, it was women being bitchy to me. By the time I completed my first enlistment, I had already been approved by the Pentagon Air Force to do a publication for *Maxim* and had been featured on *Sports Illustrated*'s website. I found making friends with the women on base was pretty hard for me, but for some reason, I always had better luck with the women at Jake's unit.

I would see them at functions, and we instantly had the military woman connection. We were able to bond over similar circumstances, especially bitchy women, being that a majority of the time, they were receiving some form of harassment from the spouses. These women were just like me. They were strong, liked to work out, typically pretty independent, and were usually taking a few college classes on the side.

What I started noticing is that no matter where we were stationed, whether it was at our STS or the other bases we were assigned to, it became very evident early on that some of the spouses were threatened by the female support personnel at the STSs simply because they worked with their husbands.

In one instance, one of the wives of a higher-ranking enlisted sergeant took it upon herself to spread a rumor that the physical therapist was having an inappropriate relationship with one of the married guys that she was working on. It was a straight-up vicious lie. For one, the physical therapist was in the military herself and would not risk her job or facing sexual harassment charges by doing something like that. Two, she was engaged to an officer at the unit. Her only fault was that she was attractive. She was also more than qualified to do her job and extremely educated—in other words, a triple threat. All this rumor ended up doing was starting a ton of drama at the unit. It ended up with the entire unit in chaos for a good couple of months.

Now, knowing what I just explained about how words and reputations travel fast in the military, could you imagine how harmful that was to her career long-term? In another absurd instance, a few of the wives did not like that my friend, a medic, had a rather large Instagram following. The entire time she was deployed, they would stalk her on social media and report back to her chain of command, attempting to get her in trouble for taking selfies with or without her coworkers. It then escalated to one of the wives taking it upon herself to go to the actual unit one Monday morning and tell her that she was wearing too much makeup in uniform.

Think about that for a moment. A wife with zero military affiliation, coming into a military workplace and having the audacity to tell a military member, who just so happens to work with her husband, about how she should do her makeup and what she should post? This is what you call wearing your husband's rank or wearing their beret. Just because you are married to a military member does not mean that you yourself are a military member, and just because you are married to a special operator does not mean you have any special status. Success is not sexually transmitted.

The mentality of looking down on other women and gossiping among themselves is an unfortunately all-too-common occurrence across the entire military but seemed amplified in the special tactics community, especially among the younger spouses. They think that because they are married to a controller or pararescueman, they are better than the girlfriends. What I came to find out after spending almost a decade in the special tactics community and having a very successful marriage is that it was usually the women that were the angriest and vicious to other women that were being cheated on, unbeknownst to them.

In some cases, if they did know, they would willingly turn a blind eye to it because they wanted the affiliation within the community. They wouldn't let anything get in the way of their wife status regardless of how miserable their marriages became. This woman was usually divorced out of the community by year five of marriage. Seeing them treat other women the way they did made it really hard to not blurt out the truth. This was especially true when they were mean to Ace.

Eventually, after showing up to a few squadron functions with Jake, I was suckered into attending a spouses' meeting. Had his chief's wife not asked me directly why I wasn't attending, I probably would have continued to avoid them altogether. Based on what I observed these women say and do and the horror stories I listened to from the men they were married to, I was dreading attending. It wasn't until I attended my first meeting that I realized that most of the women in attendance only cared about gossiping, showing off their rendition of last season's Tory Burch shoes, and the designer bags that they pestered their husbands to buy them with their bonuses or deployment money.

"Have you heard about Jessica?" one of the women said.

"Oh yes, the poor thing," another said. "I would have been so embarrassed."

"Good thing Jonathan isn't like that," another woman said. "Look what he got me for our anniversary." She held out her hand, all sausage fingers spread. On her middle finger was a large emerald-cut ruby.

"You are so lucky," another girl said. "All I got for our anniversary was this." She held up a brown tote bag and ran her hand across the monogrammed LV.

"Wait, what happened to Jessica?" another woman asked.

"Oh, you didn't hear?"

They all reminded me of hens. They would pick at anything to include themselves, and cluck-cluck-cluck all day long. The only time they would shut up is when the chief or commander's wife would walk by. They would pretend to be sweet and kiss ass, and the moment she was out of earshot, it was back to clucking. It was here that I realized, even among the wives, there is a need to one-up the other, whether it was with purses or wedding rings. The last impression I was left with was a sense of materialism that was unfounded.

What I could never figure out is how someone could spend their husband's money on a designer bag that costs half a month of their husband's salary. Everyone knows how much the spouse is making because income is based on rank. Or why would they have their husband finance a wedding ring that is more expensive than his car? Maybe it's because I realized after I joined that buying a designer bag was not worth spending half your paycheck on. It was never hard to tell whose husband had just re-enlisted at the spouses' meetings. There would always be a new bag or a new fiancée with a financed wedding ring. I realized it was a simple mindset with these women, and that level of materialism was something I couldn't deal with. I got home shell-shocked and pretty much word-vomited to Jake about my experience.

He roared with laughter. "You actually went?"

"Yeah, I just wanted to check it out, see if there was anyone worth making friends with."

"And?" he asked.

"*Nada,*" I said.

He was surprised that I found nothing of worth at the meeting. I will say this, if you want a successful marriage to any Type A dude, you have to have your own life, your own career, and bring something to the table. You have to have some form of ambition if you expect the marriage to go well. These guys are attracted to drive, success, and Type A women in general. You can't pretend to be something you're not. If you don't have something to offer, you'll just end up another divorce statistic in the family resiliency training slides.

My final straw with the spouses' club came rather quick the summer of Jake's fourth deployment. There was a couple named the Elders. SSgt. Elder and Evelyn had three beautiful little girls together. They had been one of the few couples that both Jake and I had known since the beginning of his pipeline. They started having trouble after SSgt. Elder's third deployment. He hit an improvised explosive device (IED) on a convoy and gotten blown up, among a few other things, including having his entire team ambushed. Evelyn had always been very active at spouses' luncheons. She was a very sweet, small-town, southern girl who married very young.

It was at this luncheon that she very publicly broke down about her marriage in front of not only the other spouses, but also the entire chain of command. As she stood there and hit her breaking point, crying and yelling about what she was going through in her marriage, they all snickered and made snarky comments.

"I can't take it anymore," she yelled. "I don't know what to do. I've tried everything. His drinking is becoming worse. He can't sleep at night. Do you even know how long it's been since I was able to get a full night's sleep? And the girls. I don't want them to see their father like this and y'all keep deploying him!" She hunched over and shuddered. Her tears were no longer silent.

"Well, maybe if she was more supportive of her husband," I heard a girl whisper. I tried to contain my fury, but I hit my own breaking point.

"Are you f**king kidding me right now? That's all you can say? What the hell is wrong with you?" The girl shut her mouth.

"What am I supposed to tell the girls?" Evelyn put her face into her hands.

As she continued to cry convulsively, the other spouses passed judgment about what was wrong with her and her marriage and proceeded to laugh about it after she rushed out of the event. I was disgusted. I called Evelyn later that night to make sure she was okay, but quickly realized her marriage was over and there was not much that I could do.

Evelyn and SSgt. Elder ended up divorcing a year later. He had post-traumatic stress disorder (PTSD), but it was intentionally overlooked. Evelyn tried everything she could do to keep the marriage together. She contacted his chain of command and spoke to the unit family psychologist and the chaplain, but eventually, the work tempo and the lack of him being home resulted in his marriage ending. It was that day that I decided that unless Wonder Woman herself became a wife of one of the guys, I wanted nothing to do with the group that frequented the spouses' club, and I never went to another event again.

Instances like the Elders were not uncommon. It was typically worse for the younger marriages versus the couples that have been in the career field for more than six years, but even then, some of the things you hear could be a screenplay from *Days of Our Lives*.

We eventually both got tired of it. It was easier to have a peaceful life away from the mess of what relationships became at an active-duty STS. The older we got, the more we became comfortable with being private in our personal life and having a life away from the team. Jake and I both learned that when you get to a new unit, the married couples that are chill would tend to give you some subtle heads up as to whom to avoid. It's an old boy system that you very much want to be a part of.

The last thing a special tactics unit, or the community in general, needs is a bunch of entitled wives that think they run the show. These women are not the true face of the controller or pararescueman's wife. There is an absolute difference between the wives who have been married into the community for seven or more years and those that are not. The true controller and pararescuemen's wives are humble. They are strong and selfless. They, without question, hold down the home and provide a backbone not only for their marriages, but also for the community. The true wife offers quiet support when it gets tough. And I promise you these times will come with every deployment cycle.

The one thing I did learn very early on was, after the first deployment, these men don't give a shit about what anyone does on Facebook or Instagram. They don't care about how much makeup someone should wear at work or if someone is technically a "wife" or not. They don't care anymore about who is dating who. They have seen a world that exists outside of our comfort bubble. It forever changes them, and eventually, it changes the ones they are married to.

CHAPTER 8

The First Deployment

FOR YEARS, UP UNTIL JAKE went to his first STS, all he did was learn his job. It was all training up until this point. On Jake's first deployment, I didn't really know what to expect. All I knew is that he was going to Afghanistan. Yes, I was in the military, but my military and Jake's military were two different things. People that I worked with deployed to a nice base that had a Cinnabon and Starbucks, but Jake deployed to a base that was outside your average conventional military base.

Jake's first deployment came on super short notice, and by that, I mean he had gotten a call two nights prior that he would have to leave in the next forty-eight hours. I didn't even have time to adjust to the idea of him leaving. It came with the territory, though. You really do marry the job when you end up with one of these guys.

The day I dropped him off, I fought like hell to hold back tears. I knew the last thing I wanted him to remember before he left for six months was me crying. The reality of his job started to settle in. It was no longer partying. My life was Florida beaches, nine-to-five military work, and "Hooyah Air Force." I knew that he would be going to a very dangerous place.

Since it was such short notice, I had to drop him off at our local airport, meaning he was flying civilian. The one perk to this was that deployments were a common occurrence to the airport staff at our local airport, so they allowed family members to walk deploying military members back to their terminal. Prior to me being given my family pass to escort Jake, Jake had to check in at the airline counter for his ticket. He also had to check his pelican case and deployment bag. His pelican case was a MASSIVE black hard plastic case that you could drop from a ten-story building, and it would probably be alright! It had everything he needed to do his job down range, and even looking at it from the outside, you knew there was something interesting inside. As the airline employee called Jake up to the kiosk, he asked Jake to open his case so TSA could inspect it prior to them securing the items. Although this may have been a routine inspection for this airport, you could tell most people in line had not experienced this before. Due to the items that are in the pelican cases, TSA and the service member that the gear has been issued to typically inspect the items prior to the flight and after arrival to make sure nothing has been stolen. That is exactly what Jake was doing. At this point, there were about twenty people lined up behind us and as Jake bent over to open the case he smirked.

The moment he unhinged the clasps and lifted the case open, the eyes of every man in line, including the airport employee, widened to the size of two softballs. I looked down, and there it was in front of me, all nicely cleaned and organized. Jake's war equipment. His case was complete with a suppressed M4 rifle, a suppressed SCAR heavy rifle, and a 40MM grenade launcher.

I've always wondered what the other people on his flight thought. He looked like James Bond with that amount of firepower. We passed through security, and I waited with him for the entire two hours before they announced his final boarding call. My body felt heavy as I got up to hug him. I buried my face in his shoulder so he couldn't see me tear up and gave him a big hug.

"I'll see you again soon," I said, trying to smile. Come hell or high water, I was not going to let him see the internal wreck I was.

"Hopefully," he said as he took me in his arms.

"Don't say that," I tried to reassure him. "Six months will go by in a breeze."

"I'll miss you like hell," he said, breathing into my hair.

"I will too," I said. "Call when you can. I'll be waiting for you."

"Don't get carried away by any other knights in shining armor."

I laughed despite the situation. "I wouldn't dream of it." I grabbed his big hands and pulled him in for a kiss. I tried to control the desperation that came through, but I don't know if I had succeeded. He dropped one of my hands and reached for his pack. He gave my other hand one last squeeze and reluctantly let go. I watched his back as he walked toward the terminal. I couldn't let myself break down just yet. *Don't turn around*, I thought to myself. I didn't know what kind of expression was on my face, but I didn't want him to see it. I saw him hesitate. I tried to put a smile on, but a tear escaped. He smiled a big goofy grin and waved his hand above his head like a maniac. I laughed as the tears rolled down my cheeks. I was already past the point of control. I watched him walk onto his plane, and right as I was about to turn on the waterworks, an older man approached me. What I didn't know is that he was the retired commander of Eglin Air Force Base.

He introduced himself, put his hand on my shoulder, and said, "Thank you for all you do."

And then I lost it.

I very slowly walked back to my car. Six months is a really long time to go without seeing someone you love, but it's a whole other ball game when someone is getting into gunfights during those six months. Before, I had really tried to push away these feelings. I had seen countless military homecomings because of my job in the military. I worked on the flight line, so I had front row seats to them. They never made me sad. I was always happy to see the families reunited, but to date, this was one of the hardest things I've ever had to continuously do.

What's interesting about combat controllers regarding their training is they receive the same training Green Berets, Navy Seals, and MARSOC go through. They must be able to attach onto any special operations team and handle the mission that is given. They are the least talked about branch of all the special operations divisions, yet they are the most highly trained and most expensive to produce. They pride themselves on the title of being "quiet professionals."

The training invested in one combat controller is upwards of $1 million. By the time they end training, they are considered a living, breathing tool of war. During this particular deployment, Jake was attached to a Green Beret team from the 7th Group, the closest of the army's special forces teams to Hurlburt Field. Early that summer, the army had moved their entire group to an annex of Eglin Air Force Base. Although they were only about a forty-five-minute drive from Hurlburt, they were very much so their own beast.

I was able to talk to Jake all the way until he got to Germany, which was the last transition point before he headed to his location. After that, I didn't hear from him for a few days. Once he got settled in at his forward operating base, he was able to use one of the computers to contact me. Some of the team guys managed to get internet and set it up so they could call home to their families on Skype.

They had to be careful with the internet, especially Wi-Fi, for security reasons. Even now, I am incredibly grateful for that damn app. I have no idea how women and families did deployments during previous wars, especially World War II or Desert Storm. I always felt lucky that at least I could see Jake's face and talk to him.

We hadn't been talking for more than five minutes during the first Skype call when I heard the mini-gun blasting in the background. It was surreal. You see this happen in movies, but it's a lot different when you are sitting in your house and you're trying to have a conversation with your husband. Later on, I found out they were firing at an al-Qaeda member who had approached the forward operating base head-on with a vehicle loaded with explosives. They call them VBIEDs, or vehicle-borne improvised explosive devices. Needless to say, that phone call was quickly cut short. The extremist was killed and his entire vehicle detonated only a few hundred yards from the front entrance of their base.

It was at this point that I had an "oh shit" moment. Here I was in sunny, tropical Florida, the spring break capital of the United States, hearing the spouses bitch about other women, and the love of my life was getting shot at, and someone had just tried to kill his team with a vehicle loaded with explosives. I talked myself through that phone call, and from then on, I didn't care how bad my day was. Whatever issues I had going on in my life while he was deployed did not get passed on during our Skype sessions. I knew that with everything Jake had going on, the last thing he needed was to be stressed out or concerned with all the pointless crap at home.

In this job, during the deployments, your home life and relationship need to be stable. What I found is, if there is a good home life and a good relationship, the guy will think about it a lot when they are alone and deployed. It gives them something to look forward to, to fight for, and to come home to. It was because of this that I would put on a smile, let him know that I was okay and that I loved him, and tell him nothing but positive and good news from home. Period.

With Jake in Afghanistan, I learned how to get creative with the deployment boxes I sent him. If you haven't checked out Pinterest, you need to. Now, I am personally not much of a "Suzie Homemaker," but there are definitely those of us out there that are. And thank God for them and their blogging skills. It was on Pinterest that I found a plethora of deployment box ideas, decorating ideas, and instructions for how to make cakes in a jar.

I would send a different themed box to him on Saturday morning, every two weeks. I started with an America theme and moved onto gag gifts, movie themes, and pretty much whatever I could think of that would bring some color into his world. I became a regular at the local craft store, buying everything from scrapbooking items to glitter to fart putty.

I never really reflected on how special it was that Jake and I had been friends prior to dating until our first deployment. It was this same friendship that carried us through all of our deployments. There was never an awkward moment of silence or lack of things to talk about when he was gone. If I was working, he was texting me on Skype. No phone call or message ever went unread or un-replied to, even if we were mad at one another.

I won't sit here and tell you that we didn't have small disagreements when he was deployed. We definitely did. I think one in particular was over getting another dog. Nonetheless, they only ever lasted a few minutes, and we had an unbreakable promise to never ignore one another, even when mad. You cannot do that to someone who is deployed. Skype is your new and only lifeline. If you want to maintain your relationship, you honor the "thou shall not ignore" commandment.

We started watching shows and movies together on DVD that he couldn't get in-country and talking about my schooling, life, and goals. With the time difference, we found scheduling when he would call was a lot easier than running the risk of missing a phone call. When we did this, I would be expecting him, in a quiet place with good Wi-Fi and the availability to talk. Missed calls were always a terrible feeling because I didn't know when he would be able to talk to me again, and internet was not always guaranteed.

In fact, the internet went out a lot, and during his last deployment, I caved and opened up a new cell line to get him a mobile hotspot that came in handy more than a few times. I also made sure to request the night shift at work on base so that I was on the same schedule as him. My request was automatically obliged since most of my coworkers were married and had kids. If I worked the night shift, they could be with their families, and I could be with mine. It was an automatic win-win.

All of these adjustments made us feel better about the entire situation, especially Jake. Although he was deployed, and it was part of his job, I know he felt good knowing that I was able to talk to him often and that I wasn't completely writing him off since he was gone. It was something that we were both very much so doing together. I had seen the amount of training he had gone through during his time at the STTS. I knew that he had been highly trained to do his job and that when they were deployed, they always had air support and eyes on them, regardless of the mission they were on. That was important. That factor alone was a guarantee that Jake had the upper hand in most situations. I had to trust in him and the people around him.

He was smart, well-liked, and "squared away," as they say. I never doubted that he would be okay. I also had, and still have, a huge amount of faith in the overseas leadership of these guys. The loyalty of the leadership to these men is unseen anywhere else. Heaven forbid anything did happen to Jake, I knew they would move heaven and earth to get him out of there or get them the support he needed to stay safe and alive.

I intentionally stayed busy every day to pass the time. Within the first two months of him being gone, I had completely rearranged my furniture, redecorated the house, color-coordinated and organized our closets, painted a painting of Mt. Rainer on a huge-ass canvas, and made slipcovers for our sofas. After I was satisfied with my home décor, I decided that I needed to get a bit more creative with my schedule to pass the time. Maybe I was becoming a "Suzie Homemaker" myself. I decided to start investing time in my gym routine, school, and friends, and I pestered my family to come visit. Before I knew it, I got the phone call from Jake telling me his replacement would be there in a month to switch him out. I'm sure any military girlfriend or wife would agree that this is what we look forward to the entire time they are away. Those few little words will put pep in anyone's step.

I found out a few days later that I was being sent to Mississippi for a military training mission for a few weeks. I knew it would be cutting it close, but I didn't have a choice, and I was supposed to come back home before him anyways. I headed off to Mississippi with my supervisor later that week. They had us staying on base, and I was working a pretty light workload. It was more of a vacation than anything.

Ace called me not even a week after I had been on temporary duty to tell me she had broken up with Roger, the controller she was dating and Jake's teammate. Although I tried to console her, the truth was I was completely ecstatic that they had broken up. He was the biggest asshole in the world and a serial cheater. A month prior, I had gone with Ace to her boyfriend's house for dinner. He had been drinking, but that shouldn't be an excuse.

"I know you're cheating on me, you b*tch," he yelled.

"You know I am not. I love you, baby," Ace said.

"Yeah right. All lies." Roger said. He pointed a grubby finger at her. "Big mouth, big ass, big thighs." He snorted. No one laughed with him. I didn't just feel bad for Ace, I literally hated Roger. He was abusive.

"Baby, don't be like that." She tried to put a hand on his shoulder. He smacked it away.

"Get out of my house, ham hocks," he yelled.

"Baby," she pleaded.

"Get the f**k out," he yelled. He reached for another beer and chugged it, throwing the empty can toward her.

She took a deep breath and walked out of the house. Not a single tear. She was used to it, and that was sad. Our friendship started to crumble after that night because we started to fight about him. She was my best friend. A sister. We served together, supported one another, and here is this asshole was absolutely shitting on her. He was cheating on her, told her she was fat, stupid, ugly. You name it, he said it.

During my TDY, Ace drove out and stayed with me for a weekend. Coincidently, her ex, a controller at one of the other units, also happened to be at the same training exercise my unit was partaking in. She conveniently ran into him a few times, and it raised her spirits. After she left, I went back to work, and eventually, I got a phone call from Jake saying that he was coming home early. He was projected to come back the day my training mission was ending, and I was easily a six-hour drive from base in Mississippi. I very quickly called my supervisor and told him about Jake. My supervisor was a huge, African American man from Compton. To this day, he has been the best damn supervisor I have had in the military.

He would always tease me and call me Olive Oyl because of how skinny I was. I knew he would have my back if I asked to leave the exercise early to get Jake. The exercise ended at 10 AM, and it was only about an hour flight back to Florida from Mississippi, but the problem was we were driving. My supervisor agreed to drive my equipment back with him to base if I could sweet-talk one of the pilots into letting me fly Space-A back to base on one of the aircraft. I sprinted to the nearby flying unit and begged the aircraft commander to let me hop on the next gunship back home with them.

"Look, sir, I don't mean to be rude, but I haven't seen my husband is six months. He is a controller at the STS and is getting back from deployment at 1330. I have nothing with me. I need to get on that plane home."

And that, ladies and gentlemen, is how you get shit done in the military. He smiled and let me right on that aircraft. As soon as we landed, I had to figure out how I was getting home. Granted, I was three miles from base, but I had no ride, and it was already almost noon. I didn't have time to walk home, and I needed to get to my car in order to be able to pick up Jake.

All of our buddies were TDY, Ace was working, and taxis couldn't get on base. So, I came up with the next best solution: call one of the dudes at my unit for a ride. I had never talked to the guy, but I knew he had a crush on me. Desperate times call for desperate measures. Less than three minutes later, he picked me up, and I was on my way home. I was in crunch mode. There was so much to do and not enough time. The house was a mess. I had no food for him in the fridge since I had been gone and wasn't expecting him for another week. And to make matters worse, I was absolutely disgusting and sweaty. I smelled like aircraft fuel, I was still in uniform, and most importantly, I hadn't bothered shaving my legs for most of the time he was gone, because what's the point? I was on the verge of resembling Sasquatch's cuter little sister.

All I could think of was how upset he would be if he got off that bus and I wasn't there. I still don't know how the hell

I managed to pull it off, but I took a shower, shaved, did my makeup and hair, got dressed, cleaned the house, and hauled over to an Arby's to grab him a shake and burger. I figured after flying directly from Germany, he would be hungry. I managed to get to the homecoming location all in a span of an hour and a half.

I peeled into the parking lot exactly fifteen minutes before Jake got there, only to find that most of the wives appeared as though they had spent the entire morning getting ready and were about to head to prom. They were all in heels and dresses. As I got out of my car to walk over to the area where the deployment buses would bring the guys, I saw a few of the wives taking shots of whiskey in the back of one of their cars to avoid the awkwardness. Six months makes anyone nervous to see their loved one again, especially when you are about 90 percent sure you're about to shag. It's a ton of different emotions, so I guess the whiskey took the edge off.

Looking back, I probably should have taken one myself because I was all disheveled. I felt like a total jackass. I was in jeans, a tank, and Converse shoes, holding an Arby's bag. It must have been pretty comical in comparison. My favorite part of the entire homecoming is always the little kids holding the signs for their dads. That in itself will bring any big badass dude to his knees. There is nothing more heartwarming than seeing a child see their dad for the first time in months.

I had been there for no more than ten minutes when the chaplain stood up on a chair and yelled, "FIVE MINUTES OUT!" Everyone squealed, and the kids yelled in excitement. The big white buses began turning the corner into the squadron parking lot. All eight of them lined up behind one another, and the guys started coming off. The moment I saw

Jake peek his head out of the bus, I could see he was looking for me. Right behind him was Jonas, of course. I could see that he didn't see me and saw his face drop. Being that I was in Chucks, I didn't have to worry about falling on my face in comparison to the heeled wives, so I hauled ass over to him and jumped him, Arby's bag and all.

Jake knew I had been in Mississippi, but he didn't know if I was going to be back in time for when he got off that bus. The last we spoke, the aircraft was refueling at McGuire Air Force Base in New Jersey, and I told him I was going to try my best to be there. He wrapped me in his arms and picked me up. He was so warm. He was smiling from ear to ear. I could feel him sigh in relief.

"I missed you so much," I choked out in between sniffles.

"I did too," he smiled.

I squeezed my arms around his neck. It felt like, no matter how close our bodies were, it still wasn't close enough. I wanted us to melt together so that nothing could ever separate us again. I was happy, relieved, and thankful. It felt a little like a mild heart attack.

To spend all that time apart, to spend so many moments alone and unsure, and then to, all of a sudden, have that person you have spent months missing right in front of you is a weird feeling. It feels like life is being breathed back into you, and you didn't even realize how dead you had been.

I thought that I wouldn't cry, but I was quickly proved wrong, and I was happy that I came prepared in advance. My solution for "happy tears" was a pair of big sunglasses and the "face-to-shoulder" hug technique. If you tear up, you have to hide the ugly cry face. This allows you the very crucial few seconds where you partially want to cry like a baby that the love of your life is back home safely but you don't want to show everyone else that you're being emotional. I've always been pretty private about that type of thing. Once you regain your cool again, you can pull back from the hug. Works like a charm every time.

The entire ride home, Jake just stared at me, held my hand, and smiled. I didn't know if he wanted to eat me or snuggle me; either would have been fine. I was already very shy around him, and it actually took me a few years to finally be able to make eye contact with him. Once he asked me why I could never look him in the eye. He said, "For the longest time, I couldn't read you. I didn't even know if you liked me and why you couldn't make eye contact, but I knew you had to because you married me."

He has been the only man to ever look into my eyes the way you look through a clear window. He has been the only man to see me for exactly who I am. Through all of his deployments, that feeling never went away. It is always the same ride home.

CHAPTER 9

I Promise You, You Can't Make This Up...

I HAD HEARD RUMORS ABOUT THE things that happened when the guys were on their way back, but I didn't actually believe them. I was quite happy in my ignorance until Jonas word-vomited his ménage à trois experience one day while we were out. Call me naïve, but it never crossed my mind that that would be on a to-do list when you were on your way home from a deployment, especially in Germany of all places. The only thing I could think of was the scene from *Full Metal Jacket* where the guys are coming home from the bars. Leave it to Jonas to have that type of escapade and bring it up at dinner.

Jonas never censored anything around me. He was like a big brother that informs you on the ways of the world. Like telling you Santa Claus isn't real—not to be a jerk, but because he genuinely feels like he is doing you a service and protecting you from the disappointment of finding out your parents lied to you. That was one instance where I wish he would have just kept his mouth shut.

After I found out about the wild and unrated adventures of Jonas, Jake made it a point to always call me when he was in Germany…probably because he knew I was horrified about this once I found out. One night, Jake called me after he had gone to dinner with the guys. They had just landed in Germany and were only staying for a few days to initiate their "re-adjustment" phase. He knew I was pretty close to one of the guys' wives at the unit. They had been married for twelve years, which, in the special tactics community, was a record. When he called me, I could tell something was bothering him so I straight up just asked him what was wrong. He told me that my friend's husband had gotten wasted and was headed out to some questionable locations with some of the guys. Jake had tried to get him to go back to his room, but he wanted nothing to do with it. Jake was specific about saying he saw nothing happen, but he knew where they were headed.

It ate at me. Jake had no idea that the guys' wife, whom I was friends with, was downstairs in my living room, making a "Welcome Home" sign. I whispered into the phone that she was in our living room, and Jake said he would update me on the situation. I got off the phone, sat in my bathroom for a few minutes to think of what I was going to say, and walked downstairs.

"How's Jake? Has he seen my husband? He told me he was heading to bed. I'm so excited to see them tomorrow," she said with a smile. I knew I couldn't tell her exactly what Jake had just told me, but I had to tell her something. Drop a few breadcrumbs so that she would stumble onto the truth. As much as I wanted to blurt out what Jake had just told me,

I was not about to ruin this woman's happy moment by telling her that her husband was completely drunk and heading to somewhere he shouldn't be.

"Yeah, he did actually. Jake saw him headed out with the guys. I think they're pretty wasted. You should really call and make sure everything is okay. You know how they get. Jake said they're going out. I would DEFINITELY call him."

"No, he said he's in his room," she shrugged. I felt even worse that she had complete faith in the guy.

"Jake just told me he saw him. If it were me, I would call," I said.

I could see her body language shift. Early on in their relationship, there had been an issue with infidelity. I couldn't tell her how I knew. Nor could I tell her what I knew he was doing. But I refused to cover for him. I couldn't. If this had happened to me, I would want to know. This quickly became my biggest debacle. I knew if I told her flat out, she would tell her husband and probably stay with him anyways. He had cheated before, and she did the same thing. I also knew that there was the slim possibility that he wasn't cheating on her but there was no true way of confirming. Jake and I knew where he was headed and he was lying to her. If I told her what I knew, Jake would never hear the end of it at work. So, I did what I could to let her know her husband was out and very much so lying to her about where he was.

In fact, that same night, one of the guys that had gone out to the establishment in question got so drunk that he was unaccounted for the next day. When he did eventually return to base, it was only five hours before the aircraft was set to leave to come back to the United States. Technically, he had gone AWOL. He, of course, was married, and Jameson, their supervisor, was pissed. He made him do burpees (a terrible exercise) until he threw up. To no great surprise, married or not, there were quite a few guys who frequented the locations every time they would transition back from deployments, only to show up a few hours later, as in the instance of the guy who had gotten smoked by Jameson, at the homecomings with chocolates and teddy bears for their wives or girlfriends.

Most of the time, everyone knows who is cheating, but no one talks about it. So, there we were at dinner, and Jonas was blabbing away in great detail as to what happened on their "adventures." I was not completely shocked by this because I had seen some shady stuff firsthand. Although, it is a little disheartening that there is only a handful of guys, usually the more religious ones, who didn't cheat. Had it not been for our constant communication, I probably would have started to question Jake's loyalty—especially after seeing all of this—but the one thing that made me feel secure in knowing that he wasn't doing this was who he was hanging out with, the constant communication he had if he ever had cell service, and our level of openness. We didn't hide anything. That included me letting Jake know whenever his "teammates" would step out of line with me.

Both Jake and myself were not ever fully rid of the rumor mill as much as we both tried to avoid it. I don't know if it was because we were young and in the military, or that people were genuinely just bored, but at a few times during our relationship, people had tried to start rumors of infidelity about Jake and me. Those quickly died though. Rumors tend to do that when there isn't a foundation or evidence for them.

There were some instances where the wives did find out about the longer-lasting affairs. Sometimes it was from phone bills, or a heads up from another guy or wife at the expense of team drama, or they were contacted directly by the other woman. There were also quite a few marriages that ended during deployments because a guy would meet another military member and call off his marriage or relationship. The motto became "what happens overseas/TDY stays overseas/TDY."

That is unless you catch a STD…which did happen. Every time you get to a new duty station, you have to do an incoming airman briefing. It was to let us know about off-limit establishments, dangers in the area, and facts about the base. We not only were at a training base for the combat controllers and a few other tech schools, but we also happened to be located next to one of the biggest Air Force Bases in the country, which had its own tech schools and was in the spring break capital of the United States. The alcohol on top of that made it an STD funhouse. It wasn't uncommon to hear about someone coming down with one here and there.

The one good thing about constantly having a pararescueman on your team is the unjudged and abundant access to penicillin. Ask any PJ if he's heard of another PJ, or if he personally has ever had to give his teammate a shot for syphilis, chlamydia, or gonorrhea, and I'll bet you five dollars he has.

This was one case with a controller named Esko. He was married to another military member that worked on base, and boy was she was mean. She constantly put him down, complained, didn't want to let him do anything, hated everyone in his unit, and was just all-around a miserable person. Esko was unhappy with the marriage, but soon after they were married, she had gotten pregnant with their first child.

After about almost a year of hell incarnate, Esko headed out on a work trip where he quickly became acquainted with the local bartender. When Esko came home, everything was fine, or so he thought. His wife had found out shortly after he got back that she was expecting again. Like any normal expecting mother, she went for her routine pregnancy check-up only to be notified that she tested positive for gonorrhea. She worked on base, so she had her own doubts as to why the "mix-up" occurred in the lab with her test and someone else's. Of course, immediately after finding out about her apparent positive result, Esko freaked out and immediately asked the PJ on the team for a shot of penicillin before his wife could request that he also get tested.

She was still treated for gonorrhea nonetheless, and to prove his faithfulness, he also went to the clinic to get tested, but by this time he had already been treated. When his results came back negative…it was case closed. Unfortunately, shortly thereafter, she lost the baby. We never did find out if it was the actual cause. She never found out the truth about the STD and Esko cheating. I still wonder if he felt any remorse about the whole situation. For both Jake and me, it pretty much changed our entire interaction with him. They ended up divorcing after one more child, when he finally stopped coming home.

If this wasn't bad enough, you had to deal with the flip side of cheating: when a wife cheated on her husband while he was deployed. Being in the military, especially as a woman, I saw it from both sides. I would hear stories, not just in special operations, but from my own coworkers and in my unit, and I would also see things firsthand whenever I went out on a regular basis. The minute their husbands would leave for deployment or extended TDYs, it was game on for some of the wives.

One thing about the military that most people, even civilians, know is: we are always moving. Kids are even nicknamed "military brats" because of this. Jake and I, however, ended up being the exception. We ended up "homesteading" our assignment by chance. That meant we didn't receive orders to move to a different duty assignment and ended up being in Florida for most of our time on active duty. There was a brief time after Jake graduated from the STTS where he received orders to Pope Air Force Base in North Carolina, but my job coding kept him in Florida since there was no position available for my job at Pope. The military will code two individuals to stay together if they are married, so it ended up working out in our favor. No one ever wants to get stationed at Pope. They call Fayetteville, North Carolina, "Fayettenam" for a reason.

It was because of this that we saw a huge number of not just controllers, but many military members, along with their wives and girlfriends, and pararescuemen come and go. Some of the things we saw go on with the personal lives of these guys could rival Jerry Springer. If you have seen it on a TV drama, chances are it happened in real life at this base. It was always hard for me to get close to any of the significant others unless I knew that the guy they were with was good.

Frankly, as far as being a moral human being goes, if I'm friends with a woman and I know she's being cheated on, I'm going to tell her. If I know a guy is being shady but I don't have proof, I'll tell her to the best of the ability what I can confirm. This complicates things when you're also friends with your husband's friends and coworkers. It was for this exact reason that much of the time, it was easier to just stay away. Call it a curse or a blessing, but I happen to be an awful liar.

After Jake became a sergeant on his team, he assumed more of a supervisor role with some of the younger, incoming guys. This meant I could no longer dodge work functions anymore. So, I started attending dinners with his troops and their wives and went to the team functions. One thing I always enjoyed was the parties. If there is one group of people that know how to have a good time, it's people who are getting ready to deploy.

It was at one of these parties that I met Summer. Summer was the living embodiment of a cream puff. She was loud, blonde, big, and had a larger-than-life personality. The one thing I liked about Summer was she had no filter, which made for some hilarious entertainment, especially after she had had a few drinks. Jake happened to be her husband's supervisor, so naturally, she tried to cozy up to me. For no reason, may I add, because I genuinely don't think she realized that I had zero say or control over what rating her husband was given on his enlisted performance report (EPR).

It made it awkward at times because her husband was a pretty lively character himself and was always getting into trouble. Think bull in china shop. I didn't mind, though. She was someone you could go out and have an entertaining time with, so I gave her a chance. But it took me a few months to get comfortable hanging out with her. After her relentless calls and texts, I decided to go out and grab a drink with her one night when Jake and his team were gone for work.

It was here that she unloaded all of the crazy circumstances that she found herself in. She was a prior divorcée with one kid from another marriage, had known a ton of the guys, had moved near base from another state—a very common story actually. I still didn't care. She was very straightforward, or so I thought, and at this point, after the continuous train wrecks I would come across, I appreciated her honesty. After our very first time hanging out, I had about five of the guys and various women contact me, warning me to stay away from her. They all said she was crazy. Maybe I should have listened.

Now, as a woman, the term crazy is usually used to refer to a woman that has bad blood with a guy. For me, as a rule of thumb, I like making my own opinions. So, I made a mental note, didn't tell her anything personal, and would hang out with her to pass the time. I genuinely liked her for a while, but I could never figure out how it was that she didn't work, was operating on a military income, wore nothing but designer shoes and bags, spent $20,000 on plastic surgery, and blew money like it was nothing. That is, until she really got comfortable with me and mentioned her friends and ex-boyfriends, all of whom were easily over sixty years old.

One night, as I was sitting in my pajamas doing homework, my phone rang.

"I'm outside your house," she said.

"You're what?" I loved the spontaneity of her coming to my house, but I also questioned it because our husbands were gone on a training trip, and she had two little kids at home that she never spent time with. My red flags started popping up. I barely was able to hang up the phone before I heard a knock at my door.

"You're wearing that?" she said as I slowly opened the door. She was in a mini dress and heels with enough makeup on to rival a *RuPaul* contestant.

"Did I miss something?" I looked down at my PJs and comfy socks. I didn't think I had made plans with her. She walked around me and came inside.

"Get ready," she said as she opened her purse and popped an Adderall. "We're going out."

"I can't. I have to finish a project for school." I pointed to my spread of books on the coffee table.

She shook a finger at me, "No, no. I won't take no for an answer."

"Okay, fine," I caved. "But I can't stay out too late. I have to finish this tonight."

She smiled in victory, and I went to go get changed into something a little more "going out" acceptable. As soon as we got out, her one drink turned into five. I knew that I couldn't leave her out alone. For starters, she was married to one of Jake's troops. But secondly, she was utterly wasted.

"Well, I could go home with you," she slurred to a married couple. Their faces were a mixture of slight disgust and amusement. "We could have a good time," she said as she put her arms over the both of them. I saw the couple talking as she threw back another shot. I quickly went over and grabbed her. For the most part, I thought she was kidding, until she ditched me later on that night, and I ended up Uber-ing home alone. I felt extremely guilty from what I had just witnessed. As I was in the Uber, I called Jake and explained to him what happened. He, of course, had already known they were having marital issues. Her husband had just cheated on her in Key West during a skydiving trip. He told me to keep quiet and stay out of it. I didn't go out with her anymore after that night, but she continued to go out and continued to go home with different people, including a few Green Berets at the neighboring army base, and another controller whom she was "friends" with and who was in town from another unit in the Carolinas. By this time, I was trying to do damage control on my own reputation simply from being affiliated with her. She, at this point, didn't care who saw her cheating, and I wanted nothing to do with it.

Well, Summer, being Summer, did not like that I wasn't in her bubble anymore. So, she started talking about me, and I ignored it. Gossip is a common pastime in these communities, and it's best dealt with by simply ignoring it. The one friend I did absolutely love and also met around this time was Kiki. Kiki and I were closer than many people realized, and the entire time that this was going on, Kiki and I compared notes. By this time I was getting closer and closer to graduation, so she was my eyes and ears when I couldn't be there.

Summer finally got the hint when I stopped answering her calls and texts. For a while, she would message me on social media, but that eventually stopped too. Kiki had been out with her one night when she overheard Summer talking about stripping. Summer had admitted on a few occasions after she would have a beer or two that when she was younger, she was a "sugar baby," but when she started going home with people, she quickly appeared to be more than just a "sugar baby." By the time her husband got back from his first deployment, the entire base and town knew that she was stripping. She would drive out to Panama City and New Orleans on the weekends, make her money, and come back. But when he was in town, she pretended like it never happened.

At this point, there was already such a messy exchange of drama between those two that although everyone knew what was happening, no one wanted to get involved, so people kept their mouths shut. So, Summer kept stripping, her husband kept leaving, they both kept cheating, and no one said anything. After Jake and I moved a few months later, her husband filed for a divorce and in retaliation, she started stripping at the club right outside of base.

The one thing you can always count on in a military town is that they're small towns. Small towns never keep secrets. The truth always comes out—one way or another.

CHAPTER 10

Good Ol' Jameson

During Jake's second deployment, on the last day prior to Jake hopping on his flight home, he called to ask me a very important question.

"Hey, babe, I've got a question," he said. It was strange to hear his voice sound so cautious.

"Shoot," I said.

I heard him clear his throat, "Well, Jameson is going through a divorce, and he needs a place to crash. Is it cool if he crashes at our place for a bit?" He took a deep breath. "It'll probably only be a few days till he can get all settled and find his own place."

Obviously, I wasn't going to say no. Jameson was pretty chill, so I expected he wouldn't be too much of a pain in the ass. Plus, as far as team guys were considered, he had his shit together. Although Jonas would probably still be staying with us, I also knew that Jameson would not be anywhere near as messy as Jonas was, so I figured it would be alright. As it was,

Jonas liked our couch better than the guest room anyways. "Yeah, that's okay," I said.

"You're the best."

"You know it."

Per wife standards, I was already a veteran when it came to deployments, so I knew exactly what to expect and how to act when Jake and the guys got back. After everyone settled down, they liked to do a lot of team bonding.

I don't think it was a coincidence that they happened to make it home the day before St. Patrick's Day. I imagine, although Germany is an awesome place when it comes to drinking, that St. Patrick's Day is way better stateside, especially at an Irish pub near the beach.

It wasn't a surprise when Jameson suggested we all go out the night after they got back to meet up with some people. I didn't really like doing this because they were still winding down and somewhat on edge from their deployments. But I didn't want to be a stick in the mud, and I hadn't been out in a while. Out of respect for Jake, I didn't like going out to the bars when he was gone. I think the last thing that anyone should do is be trolling the bars when their significant other is deployed. So, we headed out the next day to have some fun at one of the best Irish pubs that I have ever been to in my life. They have thousands of one-dollar bills stapled up around the entire restaurant. It makes your eyes pop when you walk in.

Every year on St. Patrick's Day, this pub would do a huge party and serve Irish Wakes all night long. These were one of their house drinks that they would always add green food coloring to. We decided to get a table right near the left-hand side of the bar and waited for our friends, who were running a bit behind, per usual. It's like herding cats when everyone is drinking, so we decided to order some food and start without them. Of course, after two Wakes or so, we were all buzzed and having a blast when I realized that my red lipstick had come off. To avoid looking like Harley Quinn, I headed to the bathroom to fix my makeup.

When I got back, I walked the opposite way that I had initially gone and passed by the table behind us. It was a group of about five rather scrawny men. The town outside our base happened to be a travel destination, so just by looking at them, I could tell they were Europeans. Jake had his back turned to the table. The guy sitting directly behind him, not knowing that Jake was my husband, decided to comment on my ass.

"Nice arse," he said, "Want to go back to my room, and I can show you a real leprechaun?" His buddies laughed and elbowed each other while looking me up and down.

In a split second, Jake spun around, grabbed his beer, and tensed his fist up. Jameson, turned directly towards the English guy, looked him square in the face, and very coolly asked him, "Do you want to die?" with a mischievous grin.

Two tables down from us was a group of about five yoked, tattooed, and scruffy guys. Just looking at them, you could tell they were over at the neighboring Green Berets unit. They were acquaintances that we knew via mutual buddies and had seen the entire event transpire. One of them walked over to our table and said, "Hey man, if you got any problems, we're right here. If they start anything, we have your back." I instantly had an "oh shit" moment.

Transitioning, elevated heart rates, and re-adjusting flashed in my mind. These guys were all on a very extreme edge. Yeah, bad timing. Two very big dudes, within forty-eight hours of getting home from a deployment where they had more than likely killed terrorists, just heard some English punk comment on my "arse" and are more than likely going to beat him into a pulp. His "get out of jail free" card aside, I was not ready to have a fight go down.

We had all been drinking, so if we got in trouble, our superiors would think it was our fault. They would assume we were wasted and probably send us to an ADAPT program the military has. If they got in a fight, regardless of the circumstances, we were screwed, and it would automatically be our fault. Not only that, but our buddies had headed over, not to mention the table of guys from the 7th Group that were waiting for this group of Englishmen to get in Jake and Jameson's face. It was easily going to turn into a brawl that would end very badly.

I tried to assess the situation and possible ways of defusing it. I realized that I would probably have to take a hit for the team on this one. I turned around to Jake and gave him a hard look before giving him a big sloppy kiss. I sat on his lap and turned back around to the English guy and his table of mates. "Look," I said, "I'm here with him and him. These two guys just got home yesterday from deployment. You are in a military bar, and about 90 percent of the people around you are military. If you start anything, you're probably going to get you and your entire table's asses beat. To avoid this, can you please just apologize to my husband and me, and we can send your table a round of beers?"

He actually looked scared after sizing up the guys and agreed. He immediately apologized to Jake and me. No sooner did I turn back around to Jake and wave the waiter over, did the English guy's girlfriend yell something at me from the other side of the table. I couldn't quite make out what she said, but I assumed it was about her drink request, so I walked over to her to ask her what she said. Once I got within arm's reach of her, I managed to make out through the noise and her thick accent the words "*f**king c*nt!*" Then, in a split second, she reached over and pulled my hair while attempting to swing on me over the table.

As soon as that happened, the entire armistice that we had just established with the English went right out the window. Let me just start off by saying: (1) Fighting is trashy, (2) I never start fights, but (3) I sure as shit will defend myself, and I've never lost at anything. Her first mistake was grabbing my hair over a table and attacking me first. I was in the clear to defend myself. Her second big mistake was that she left her face open and guard down by holding onto my hair.

I squared up to her so quickly that Jake and Jameson didn't even have time to react. Jake was behind me and blocked by a barstool. I instantly decked her twice, two times in her nose, and felt someone pick up all 110 pounds of me by the waist. My Irish Wake was still in front of me on the table, so as I was being pulled away, I launched the Wake at the table, shattering the glass and drink over the entire table of English people. As this was happening, I managed to turn the incident into a history lesson and yelled, "You lost the first war. How does it feel to lose the second? F**k the English!" By that time, our buddies from the neighboring table surrounded the group of guys so that the bouncers couldn't get in, and the entire bar started chanting, "F**k the English. F**k the English. F**k the English."

The person who had grabbed me was the bartender. He was one of my friends and had been working there for about fifteen years. As I was getting pulled out, I saw Jameson chugging his beer. I couldn't see Jake. My friend set me down outside and said, "Take off. I'll take care of it from here." Without a question, I hauled ass about a mile down the road on the backroads to our favorite bar. I didn't get more than a mile away when I heard footsteps behind me. I turned to see Jake and Jameson running behind me, both laughing and out of breath. The only people crazy enough to be laughing in the middle of a brawl are those two.

Jake grabbed my face, half laughing, half concerned, and then looked at Jameson. "That was the most epic shit I have ever seen," he said.

"That was fun," Jameson said as he walked over to some bushes to pee.

"I'm going to buy you a drink," Jake said to me, still holding my face, inspecting it for battle wounds. Crazy as it sounded, that was exactly what I needed to calm down again. Had it been any other person to get in a fight, those two would have been completely screwed. Especially if there were tourists involved. The military takes any event with the local civilian community, especially when alcohol is involved, very seriously. I wanted to file a police report because I literally had been attacked, but I figured with what had just happened, that crazy woman probably learned her lesson: Don't attack random strangers.

Jameson ended up living with us for six months and became one of my favorite people. In the time that he ended up living with us, I really got to know him. There were many times that I would be baking in the kitchen, and Jameson, an avid closet chef, would be schooling me from the couch on how to properly let my Bundt cake cool before frosting it. It was times like these that reminded me that these guys were still human beings, regardless of the God complex that they were given on base and in the military as a whole. They were people's sons, brothers, cousins, uncles, husbands, and boyfriends. Jameson and I became good friends. It was because of the time he spent with us and how he got to know me that he would later have my back in a very fragile time of mine and Jake's relationship.

CHAPTER 11

Transitioning and Masking

THE FIRST THIRTY DAYS AFTER getting home from a deployment is known as the transition period. A medical fact that was repeated multiple times during the homecoming briefings for the spouses was that it takes the human body thirty days to wind down from any deployment, and the human heart also will elevate ten to fifteen beats per minute up to thirty days after a deployment.

They had the science to prove that these guys would be going through stuff when they got back, but it's hard to make civilian spouses understand that. Imagine being pumped up with adrenaline every day for the last six months in a different time zone, and getting shot at. It's going to put you on edge. Granted, although they are pretty close to real-life supermen, they're still human. So, thirty days is the average time it takes for them to re-adjust to what we constitute as "normal."

A big mistake many younger couples make is one partner, typically the girlfriend or wife, will want to go out within a few days of her beau getting home. This is a big no-no for a few reasons—mainly that they are still getting adjusted, and the last thing you want to do is bring them into a stressful, loud, and unpredictable environment, especially when alcohol is involved. It's like throwing gasoline onto a fire.

The unit will even go as far as to give each guy a small note to carry with them for the one month that they're on leave. It states in so many words, "This military member has recently come home from deployment." At first, looking at Jake's, I started laughing. An Air Force memorandum instructing "whomever it concerns to contact the military police and first sergeant at this number" in case they receive this letter from the incarcerated military member. Almost like a "get out of jail free" card. It wasn't until I realized why that letter had to be written and handed out that I realized why they did it.

I knew Jake was adjusting to being home again because his sleep schedule was off, and he wanted more quiet time than usual. But for the most part, it seemed like his first deployment wasn't too bad for him. He mentioned little things here and there about some of the guys he worked with, but all in all, he was pretty quiet about everything that had happened. In fact, he became really good friends with an army captain that was in charge of his team. They continued their friendship until the captain later transferred to the Pentagon, but we ended up spending much of that summer out with him, and only then was I able to visualize and piece together a bit more of what his deployment was like from excerpts of drunken stories.

Within the first few days of the guys getting home from deployment before they are released to go on leave, they are psychologically and physically screened at the unit. Ninety percent of the time, they will give bullshit answers to the questions the doctors, chaplains, and shrinks ask them so they can get home to their family or friends and get as far away from work as possible. You have to give the resiliency team credit for trying, but at the end of the day, these guys just want to get away from work and decompress from the stress of the deployment. It was after this screening week during Jake's first deployment that I realized Jonas had no one to go home to.

Everyone typically scatters to the winds for a few weeks on commander's time off once they're given the all-clear. Jonas wasn't shy about sharing that he had been on his own from the time he was thirteen years old. His parents had never been in the picture, being alcoholics, and an older sibling had raised him. For people like Jonas, the military gave him the structure and family that he had never had, and if there is one thing the military taught us all, it is that you are family. There was never a question in either of our minds as to whether or not Jonas could stay with us, especially after deployment.

It stayed this way for three consecutive deployments. The day they both got home, Jonas knew to come over for dinner. He would stay the night and knew the guest room was his if he wanted it. One day would turn into the next, and before we knew it, he would end up staying with us during the entire time while everyone else was on commander's time off (CTO).

After the few weeks are over, everyone cycles back to the unit, jumps right back into training, and starts preparing for the next deployment in five months. The cycle is like clockwork and never changes. A one-to-one ratio of six months home and six months deployed. Six months in a shithole, one month to "normalize," five months to get attached to your family and continuously train, and then you do it all over again.

The guys that had families were able to assimilate better than those that did not. For men like this, sometimes it takes someone you love to push back and remind you what "normal" behavior is. It was after that first deployment, followed by the second, that I started to see changes in our friends. I don't know what it was about me, but eventually, by the time we had moved from Florida, I had seen every single one of our friends cry or tear up at some point when they were drunk talking about the deployments. Maybe it was because I reminded them of a calm time or because they knew that I would never tell anyone what I was told, but their stories forever changed me and my perspective of the world. The things they saw, the things they went through. Even the strongest men will cry.

It was in teammates like Jonas that we saw the most drastic changes. The ones that didn't have their families around, or even serious relationships, to stabilize them were affected the most. With Jonas, it progressively got worse with each deployment. During his first deployment, his team sergeant was killed. During his second deployment, one of the army guys on his team was killed, and he hit an IED, which resulted in him getting a pretty bad brain injury. During his third deployment, again, his team leader got killed. It was an accumulation of the events that occurred during each of his deployments that, eventually, resulted in us losing Jonas to PTSD.

Jake and I both fought hard to bring him back to who he once was. But after that third deployment, he came back forever changed. What started out as a welcome home dinner and light conversation resulted in Jonas snapping. I had said something that triggered a memory for him, and he yelled at me. Jonas was like my brother, and although he apologized later that night, I realized something was off. During that month that he stayed with us, he started drinking heavily. He even tried to fight Jake a few times. And we eventually had to ask him to leave.

For almost a year, we struggled to get Jonas back on track, but by the time we left Florida, Jonas's occasional drinking had turned into substance abuse issues. He was functioning at work, but that was the only time he was sober. He no longer cared about the random drug testing or the people he considered his family.

Some of the guys tried to help him, but they were afraid if they pushed him too far, he would truly go off the deep end. If they asked for help at his work, he would possibly get kicked out of the military, and as f**ked up as he was, work was the only thing keeping him sane. He no longer came around to hang out with us unless it could serve a purpose for him. He would constantly ask me if I knew people at school who sold Adderall and eventually spent the majority of his free time chasing down cocaine.

Some years later, when Jake was talking to a director of one of the non-profits I worked with, I overheard Jake say, "I lost my best friend, Jonas, to PTSD. Sometimes I miss him, but the man I knew is gone." Jonas eventually ended up leaving the military, and even now, we hear from him from time to time. But it was this experience with Jonas that made me realize how soldiers masked their memories.

As the years went on, listening to conversations about the deployments and hearing about men playing *Call of Duty* and doing ketamine was not a surprise anymore. Hearing about someone looking for drugs on the weekend, about the heavy drinking and divorces, and in some cases, men up and leaving their families after deployment became common.

They transitioned home and, for some time, could mask what they experienced, but just like anything else in life, eventually, things build up and will, in one way or another, show their face. Whether it was drugs, alcohol, or running from their families, masking proved to be the hardest thing to watch.

CHAPTER 12

A 4 AM Phone Call

THE SUMMER AFTER JAKE HAD gotten back went super quick. Once the beach warmed up, we were at the beach every single weekend. Because of where we were stationed, there was no reason to vacation anywhere else. We had our secret beach spots where we would hide from our friends for quiet time every now and then. Our own little paradise. We would lay on the warm white sand. Between the warmth of the sand, the heat from Jake's body, and the sunshine falling onto us, I felt like I could melt. He would stroke my hair as the crystal blue waves lapped at our toes like a lullaby. I breathed in the scent of his skin. He smelled like beach and piña coladas. If I could put the word happiness into one scene, it would be this. My heart was so full, it felt like it would burst from my chest like in an *Alien* movie.

Towards the end of summer, I noticed I had changed. Ms. Independent, "don't need no man," working hard, going to school, super busy, got clingy. I didn't realize why until I had a self-reflection moment one day driving home from the gym. Jake had called me to say he was heading home. I was at the gym on base, so I knew if I left then that we would get home at the same time.

I very happily bolted to the locker room, even though I had just gotten there and taken my pre-workout. As I was driving, I realized I was totally whipped. Now, for someone like myself, this was immediately an inner struggle. As I was driving and trying to figure out how I became so attached, I realized Jake had told me a few weeks earlier that he would find out soon when he was deploying again. It was something I had in the back of my mind but chose to not really address till it was closer to the time he left. It was eating at me.

It is incredibly hard loving someone so much and having them leave every six months for half a year. It was worse knowing that it was very likely that during this time, some stranger in some foreign land would be trying to kill the one person you couldn't imagine breathing without.

When I got home, he was pretty excited. He scooped me up and lifted me in the air like a child. "I know where I am going," he said with a huge grin.

"What do you mean?" I barely had time to set my gym bag down.

"For my next deployment."

"Oh." I'll never understand the rush these guys get knowing that they are going to get into gunfights, but for someone like Jake, you couldn't buy any kind of contraband to compare to the highs he got when he was deployed.

I was not happy. He had heard that it was a pretty kinetic area, so he would have a busy mission set while he was there, which, for him, meant that six months would pass in no time. The day he would be leaving finally rolled around. We spent Christmas and New Year's together, and a week later, he was gone.

I dropped him off on base at his unit. Again, I put on a smile, gave him a hug, and pushed down the feelings that were bubbling up like a geyser in my trachea. I ran through the rules in my head to take my mind off of the slipping feeling that was starting to creep on me. Don't send them off with a sense of sadness, doubt, or guilt. Suck it up. This is just like every other deployment, I told myself. This was already our routine. But I couldn't completely swallow down. It's really f**king hard to say goodbye.

I got home and fell back into my rhythm. Gym, school, and work. I had been approved about one month prior, short notice, to separate from the military early to go to school full-time. That was one of the best-kept secrets that the military had: if you got approval from your commander, you could actually get out of your enlistment early to go to school. After my third time applying, I had finally been approved, and boy, was I stoked.

I had taken the liberty of registering for a full load of classes at the university I was attending. It was now in my junior year of college. I was a pre-med student and had Jake. Things were really starting to look up, and medical school seemed like a plausible future, not just a dream.

It had only been about ten days since Jake had left for Afghanistan, and my friend Ashley was relentless with reminding me her birthday was coming up that Friday. She had made huge plans. And of course, being one of her best friends, I could not miss her birthday. I made sure to do all my homework earlier that week so that I was able to go to her birthday dinner and party.

On Wednesday, Jake called me from his base. I was incredibly excited to talk to him, but I immediately saw a look on his face via Skype that left an uneasy feeling.

"How are things at home?" he asked.

"They are good. I finally have time to focus on school." I tried to smile through the queasy feeling in the pit of my stomach. "And it's Ashley's birthday on Friday. I am excited to be able to relax for a few days." I asked the question I was dreading to hear the answer to, "How are things over there?"

"Everyone is kind of standoffish. I guess they have had a pretty intense run here. They're pretty aggressive. I guess they've already had a few guys get messed up." Jake looked tired already. "There's a guy with a scar on his eye, and no one really talks. I guess the guy before me got pretty jacked up." He didn't have to say anything more than that for me to completely read everything and then some just by looking at him. I knew right then and there that this wasn't like the other deployments. He couldn't tell me the exact location, but I figured out the general area after bugging one of the other guys. It was not a place you wanted your loved one staying in.

"How are you, though?" I asked, trying not to sound overly concerned. At this point I was completely freaked out based on his reaction.

"I'm okay." I saw right through his fake smile. I hoped he didn't see through mine. "Hey, I think I have to go soon. A couple of the guys want to use the computer. I'll call you tomorrow," he said.

"Okay. Love you!" I was trying to come across as cheerful and happy as possible but I just knew something was off.

"Love you more," he said before the screen went black.

I counted the minutes until he called me again at our scheduled time. It was a short conversation. He had to go early. The whole thing made me feel even more uneasy. He called me once again early in the morning that Friday and told me he would call me as soon as he got back to base. He told me he should be back by around 6 PM my time, which was right before Ashley's birthday party. Before he hung up, he made sure to say that he loved me more than once. As much as I appreciated him telling me this, I knew something was wrong. Telling someone you love them excessively right before they are going out on a mission leaves a knot in your stomach. It's as if they expect to never tell you again.

That Friday, no matter how much I tried to distract myself, my head still went back to Jake. I thoroughly cleaned our house, did a few errands, ran a few miles, and still couldn't stop thinking about that damn mission Jake was on. Of course, it was Ashley's birthday, so she came over to my house as soon as she got off work to get ready for her birthday dinner. I tried to be happy being that it was her birthday, but she realized as soon as I opened the door that something was on my mind. Come 6 PM, I fired up my laptop and signed into Skype. I waited and waited, but there was no call. I sat there for forty minutes, and still no call.

I have never gotten so sick to my stomach, but I knew in my gut that something had happened. I was in the kitchen making dinner while Ashley talked to me, and as I turned away to the stove, I cracked. I started sobbing.

"Hey, it's okay," Ashley said, walking over to me and putting a hand on my back. She tried to calm me down.

I looked at her in the eyes and said, "Something happened to Jake. I don't know what it is, but I just know something isn't right. It doesn't feel right. I feel like he's hurt."

"You're just being paranoid. I am positive he's okay. It's just his job, just come out for a little bit and have a few drinks!" She gave me an encouraging smile.

Looking back on it, I realize she just really wanted me to come out, but I felt like she was being an asshole. Like she just wanted me to party. Like she didn't understand. When two people truly love one another, I believe God gives them a connection. Call it the red string of destiny. Call it being on the same wavelength. Jake could finish my sentences. Our communication was non-verbal. I could look at him and, in a second, know everything he was thinking and feeling without him having to utter a word.

I knew she would be mad at me, but I didn't care. "I love you, and I promise I will make it up to you," I said. "But I can't go to your birthday party."

"Yeah, it's fine. I understand," she said. Her brow was furrowed, and she seemed upset.

"I can't go to a party not knowing if my husband is safe."

"Look, you don't have to explain yourself," she told me. She gave me a hug. "When you hear from him, let me know. Maybe he will call before the party is over."

I nodded and walked her to the door. After she left, my mind started running wild. I couldn't help but run through the what-ifs in my head. Images of stark white gloves folding the American flag flashed in my mind. I couldn't let my mind go there. I tried to think about other things, anything. I stayed up all night and waited for him to call, but that call never came. All I could tell myself was "no news is good news." If he was dead, I would have been notified by now. I talked to both my parents that night, trying not to let the darkness swallow me. My head was barely above water and to add to the pressure, at this point, Jake and I had been secretly married for a few years. My mom knew, the military knew, but the rest of our family and friends back at home did not. I never envisioned myself as the type to get married, nor did I want a big wedding. In fact, I have always been very private about that type of thing...but I couldn't help but wonder, if something did happen, how would I tell everyone that we were married? By the time I fell asleep, it was three in the morning. I hadn't been sleeping for more than about an hour when my phone rang.

The TV was on the Netflix home screen. It was dark out, and my dog was passed out next to me. I reached for my phone, still half asleep, and saw a weird number. I answered to Jake's voice. I was immediately relieved but slightly upset that he didn't call me when he was supposed to.

"Hey, babe. What are you doing?" he asked.

"Oh, I don't know, sleeping," I couldn't help the sarcasm that slipped out in my voice, and I instantly regretted it. "It's four in the morning, Jake. Why didn't you call?"

"I need to tell you something," he said. "Nothing is missing, but..."

As soon as those words hit my ears, my heart stopped. I immediately sat up in bed. The house was dead silent, and the anxiety and worry wrapped themselves around me. I was going under. I could hear him take in a deep breath on the other end of the line.

"I got shot," he said. Then the phone went silent.

"Jake?" My voice was trembling. I started hyperventilating. Bile rose up from my stomach and threatened to explode. I tried to swallow it down. I looked around the room. The walls swayed back and forth as if mocking me. It felt like I was being choked by some invisible force. My eyes started to feel hot.

"Jake, please answer me," I managed to squeak out. My mind started to race a million miles an hour. I had no idea what was going on. Where the hell was Jake? He wouldn't mess around like this. Why wasn't anyone on the phone anymore? What seemed like a thousand years was only a matter of seconds.

"My God. Mrs. Finley, I'm so sorry," a man said. "This wasn't supposed to happen like this. Are you alone? Where is your family?"

"Who is this? Where are you? Where is Jake?" If I could have reached into the phone and grabbed this man by the collar, I would have. "I need to know what happened to my husband."

"Ma'am, this is Chaplain Smith of Jake's STS. I am escorting your husband. He was shot around 6 PM your time last night during an operation. He stole a phone from the nurse to call you, even though, as you are aware, this is not common reporting procedure. The reason he is not on the phone anymore is because he was given morphine just a second before he called you and is currently passed out." As I was listening to the chaplain, I knew I probably only had about a minute with the chaplain to get all the information I could.

"Where was he shot? Will he walk again?" I held my breath. I would be with Jake through anything, but I needed to know what to prepare for and I didn't want him to suffer the psychological pain that came with that kind of injury.

"He was shot in his upper right thigh," the chaplain said. "Yes, ma'am. He should be able to walk again," he sighed. "I can't believe this happened like this. I am so sorry. You will have the commander, a flight doctor, and a member of the resilience team staff at your home within the next hour. You were not supposed to find out this way. Ma'am, I am so sorry. I am so incredibly sorry. You weren't supposed to find out this way. I am so sorry."

"Sir, it's okay," I said. It felt like an elephant had been sitting on my chest and just barely decided to go on a walk. "He's going to walk. It's okay." My head was still spinning. "Please update me with his condition soon."

"Will do, ma'am."

I tried to process what had just happened. Jake had stolen a phone from one of the nurses to sneak a phone call to me while he was shot and in a hospital bed. Just to warn me ahead of time that they would be coming to my door. He knew that if I got a knock on the door at 5 AM and opened it to see his commander, the doctor, and a resiliency team member in uniform at my door, I would have collapsed. I would have thought he was dead. Jake knew this even though he was half-there mentally, so he tried to warn me.

I sat there, frozen, for about five minutes in complete shock. I was the first person on his notification list, meaning that not even his parents had been notified at this point. I gathered my thoughts and repeated to myself a few times that he was okay. He was alive and would walk. Someone had just tried to kill my husband. I tried to think about the positive. He was safe, in a hospital bed with morphine. He wasn't in pain. He was resting. This gave me a little peace of mind. I reached for my phone and called my mom.

After I told her what happened, I sat on my bed and stared at the wall. I didn't think about anything. Everything just went blank. I pulled myself together, went downstairs, and sat on the couch to wait for them to show up at my door. I stared at the door for what felt like hours until I finally heard the door knock.

I opened the door and saw the concern on their faces. They had no idea that I had already talked to Jake. To put them at ease, before they could say anything, I said, "It's okay. I already know." Instantly, the concerned looks turned to dumbfounded ones. I told them what had happened with Jake sneaking a phone call. I'm sure they were expecting the typical hysterical response because when I didn't cry and maintained my composure, they looked at me, confused. But I knew with the location of the injury that he would walk again, and frankly, I was just thankful to God that he was alive.

They eventually left. I had all the information I needed. The next order of business was how the hell could I get to Jake as soon as possible? My phone rang off the hook all day shortly thereafter. Once the unit had notified the family members, they were then allowed to release the information to everyone at the unit.

People came out of the woodwork to make sure I was okay and to let me know that they were there for me if I needed them. After a few days and an email from the commander that referred to me as a "Spartan Wife," I very quickly had shrinking patience with the fake inquiries from various wives that wanted affiliation with an injured service member's spouse.

It sounds horrendous to say, but there does exist a form of attention-seeking when someone becomes hurt at the unit or, in some cases, is killed. Many people want to be able to say they know the injured person or that they have a connection. It's like when someone is hurt, or gone, all of a sudden, all these "friends" are devastated even though they were never around before the incident. Later on, when it came down to it, I realized who really would be there for us. At the time, I had no idea how the next year would go, but it would prove to be the hardest year of my life. I didn't care to talk to anyone anymore or answer mundane texts repeating myself over and over again. I'm "fine." He's "fine." I didn't want to answer their interrogations anymore. I just wanted to get to Jake.

CHAPTER 13

Walter Reed, Maryland

I didn't eat or sleep much for the next week after finding out Jake had been shot. I had no idea what to expect, and all I was told was that they were going to try to figure out how to fly me out to see him. In my own obliviousness, I thought I would be able to keep up with my classes. I attended class that Monday, but the minute I went up to my professors to tell them what happened, I could feel my throat close up, and hot tears started to well up in my eyes. I tried to talk through what had happened but could only get out that I might miss some school due to Jake being shot.

My zoology professor thought I was making it up since we had an exam that Friday. She asked for proof that Jake had been shot. After that, the chaplain called her and gave her a piece of his mind. When I emailed her verification from the Red Cross, she replied with an apology. It didn't matter. What mattered was Jake.

Through coordination of the unit, I was flown out to Walter Reed Medical Center in Bethesda, Maryland, almost immediately to be joined with Jake once he was transferred back to the United States. Initially, I thought I would have to fly directly to Germany, but that quickly changed. The one thing I can say that the military does not do is pay for the flights of family members. Lucky for me, the unit was already working on getting a flight together for me, even if they had to pay for it out of pocket. For as much as the unit did with coordinating my flight and the hotel on base, this entire scenario was something I did very much so alone.

I didn't have any family supporting me through the process. They were all across the country with jobs and lives of their own. My friends didn't understand what I was going through. I think sometimes people don't personally know how to handle their own circumstances, let alone someone else's, and a situation like this can make them uncomfortable.

When I got to Maryland, I made my way to the car rental agency as quickly as I could. As I drove to the hospital, I could feel my heart racing at the thought of seeing Jake's face again. As I pulled up near the hospital, I saw an army amputee running with his physical therapist. It was encouraging to see yet still shocking. I hadn't even heard of Walter Reed and had no idea that it was also a rehabilitation hospital for injured service members.

As soon as I got onto base, I was instructed to call a family liaison working with Care Coalition. He was a Navy Seal that had volunteered for this position as a temporary duty. I think it was his way of giving back. It was his job to aid the family members of special operations service members who had been injured in combat. This organization within the military was set up specifically for special operators and their family members. He told me that he would come get me as soon as he received word that Jake was on the ground.

I had gotten there a few hours before Jake arrived. I managed to unpack my bag and realized immediately that I had forgotten most of the things I needed at home. I was all over the place. I wanted to cry, but I knew I couldn't. I couldn't let Jake know I was coming apart at the seams. With all he had been through already, I couldn't give him more to worry about. I sat quietly in my room, waiting for the call from the Care Coalition liaison about Jake's projected arrival time.

Eventually, I got my landing notification, and as we were driving onto base after some light conversation, the Seal turned around to me and said, "Jake's been through a lot. You may not see what I'm talking about right now, but you will. There are certain things that he is going to be going through that won't surface right now. If you can, read this book," he said as he handed me a book. I took it, although I had no idea what he was talking about. I was so concerned about just getting to Jake that I forgot the book in the car. I wish I hadn't.

He brought me to the ambulance receiving area where Jake was going to be dropped off at. I heard the sirens and saw everyone gathered around the entrance to receive Jake. My heart was pounding out of my chest. Anytime anyone tried to talk to me, they would have to repeat themselves at least three times. My brain was only focused on one thing: Jake. I only thought about one thing: Jake. I really had no idea what to expect. Although, knowing that the chaplain was there ahead of time made me feel better. I had seen him in passing down in the lobby of the hospital, and he made sure he was seen so that at least I knew I had some support.

As soon as the ambulance pulled up and the doors opened in the back, I saw Jake peek out over the covers, looking for me. It was no different than how he searched for me every time he came off the deployment busses—only, in this case, he was hurt. We immediately locked eyes, and I could see his eyes start to glaze over. He was tearing up. He put his head back and closed his eyes. I knew at that instant everything I needed to know.

He was in pain—not just physically, but in every respect. I willed my frozen legs to move and walked over to him. I gently put my arms around him and finally breathed. I didn't have the strength to do anything else except hold him in my arms.

Jake was given a hero's welcome. Most of the staff had come outside to process him in. You have to hand it to those individuals at that hospital. For the amount of chaos that they see, they still manage to put on a smile and do their job to the best of their abilities. Some of them were young airmen just like Jake and me. Which made it even more surreal. I was able to walk next to his hospital bed as they escorted him up to the room he would be in for the next few weeks.

Within the first few minutes of being inside Walter Reed, it was like a blindfold had been lifted off my eyes. It was here that I really saw what the ugly side of war looked like. It wasn't the glamorous portrayal that Hollywood painted it out to be. It was very real people in very f**ked up circumstances that left them completely in pieces. As I walked the halls one day while Jake was sleeping, I realized that most of the patients were very young. It was heavy.

The hospital was quiet except for the buzzing of machines and the occasional scurrying footsteps of a nurse or doctor. Grey. Everything was completely grey. It was like I had crossed into an alternate dimension where no color or taste or feelings lived.

One of the downsides of the drip was that it made him very tired. He slept a lot, and when he was up, he was extremely irritated. If that wasn't bad enough, everyone from the hospital, his extended family, the Pentagon, and then some were trying to come in and visit.

It was completely overwhelming for both of us. He needed quiet, and these people wouldn't stop coming in to talk. On top of this, the hospital was always freezing, and sleeping accommodations were not entirely friendly. But I did manage to arrange two large chairs to create a cot that I could put right next to Jake's bed. At one point, the chaplain decided to sit in a chair outside the hospital room door for the entire night and morning after seeing how exhausted Jake and I were. He did this so no one else would bother us. For that brief time, everyone except the hospital staff and the doctors was turned away, regardless of their rank or status. I think the president himself could have come, and the chaplain would have turned him away. It was a much-needed break.

Jake's parents had driven in from a few states away. It was overwhelming to deal with them in addition to everything else going on. We didn't talk all that much, and I didn't exactly have the best relationship with them at the time. At this time, I had power of attorney over Jake. He had made sure before he left, as part of deployment protocol, that I was given responsibility over him medically in case anything happened.

I did have to remind everyone of that when his parents and the care coalition guy suggested we do separate visiting hours. I politely but very firmly told him that Jake was my husband, and if there was going to be an issue with visitation while he is in the hospital, then there wouldn't be anyone seeing him except for me. There weren't any issues with his parents after that, but because of the tension, I reluctantly gave them time alone. I didn't want to leave him, but I knew that any stress would be bad for the healing process, and the last thing Jake needed right now was drama between me and his family. During this time, I would take walks around the hospital.

I tried not to look in the hospital rooms, but it was impossible not to. I very quickly learned that some of these patients had been there for a year, and sometimes more, in various rehabilitation programs. You could see who had been there the longest based on the amount of decorating that was in their rooms. It's already hard having a loved one in this condition, but I at least had the assurance that Jake would walk again in comparison to some of the young men and women in that hospital.

Being at Walter Reed was life-changing, and even now, I have a hard time remembering it without tearing up. After seeing eighteen- and nineteen-year-olds with multiple amputations, I was just thankful that Jake was alive. I was only a few years older than them. They were still wet behind the ears, and yet, they were dealing with these kinds of situations. The rooms were specially designed so that in the instance of limb amputation, the patients could at least pull themselves up out of bed with different apparatuses that were attached to the ceilings. It was incorporated into their physical therapy and hospital treatment plans.

The entire time I was at Walter Reed, the one person that I figured could provide me with insight as to what Jake was going through was the Care Coalition Seal. He reminded me a lot of Jameson. After seeing a few of the families in the waiting area one day, I asked him about how often he gets married couples here.

"It's common for spouses to not show up," he said frankly.

"What do you mean they don't show up?" I asked.

"Sometimes they just don't come. They say it's too much, and they don't want to deal with it," he said.

I couldn't believe it. When your loved one has been hurt, especially in war, it's really hard. Emotionally, it's a train wreck. I can understand that, but to abandon the person you love just to make it easier on yourself? That was something I couldn't swallow, especially when you promised to be with that person in sickness and in health. To treat that person even less than you would a friend, it hurt to just think about it. Younger enlisted members and officers will rush into getting married, but when the reality of marrying a military member sets in, they become one of the statistics: the spouses will think that this isn't what they signed up for and leave their spouse alone in a hospital. That is exactly why there exists some of the support networks set up in the military, for these situations.

"It's places like this that help people get through those types of situations," he said. "That's why I am here."

"I just can't imagine someone you married being hurt and not going to see them," I said.

"It's not always the wives," he told me. "About a year ago, when I first got here, we had an army member killed during deployment. His remains were brought back to Walter Reed, but when it came time for his family to be notified, we had to run down his list." He looked down and shook his head. "His wife and child showed up, along with his current girlfriend and new baby, and ex-wife." He laughed sarcastically. "He was lucky he was dead. Both women didn't know about each other. You can imagine what went down when they found out his military life insurance (SGLI) hadn't been updated to show his new wife. So, it all went to his ex."

I remember feeling like I couldn't breathe a majority of the time. When it was too much for me to bear, I found myself wandering the halls of the hospital, listening to the conversations of the staff and families. I saw the tears, the stress, and the worry on their faces and always wondered what their stories were. The stairwell was a place I had learned was usually unoccupied, unlike the prying eyes of the waiting rooms, except for the occasional happenstance when someone would have the same thoughts as me. I sat on the steps and let it take over. The worry. The uncertainty. The love. The hate. I let it wash over me. My phone rang. *Mom* flashed on the dark screen. I pressed the power button. I wasn't ready yet. To be honest, at that time, I felt like I might never be ready. After I cried until the dry heaves came, I took a deep breath. I wiped my face of the runny mascara and made sure that no hints of my breakdown were visible on my face. I tried smiling, just to test it out. I felt a stinging feeling in my throat but swallowed it down. We all have our own masks for different reasons. Mine, like my heart, was for the man in that hospital bed.

The train of visitors would eventually go away when visitation hours were over, and finally, Jake and I would have quiet time. It was a bit hard not addressing the elephant in the room, but I managed to get a few good laughs out of him referencing Forrest Gump. Initially, it pissed him off until I started talking in Forrest Gump's voice, and then, he would crack a smile. Most of the time, he was silent. He hadn't even been in the hospital for a few days, and he was already trying to walk around with his cane. Nothing would keep that man down, especially in the hospital.

Jake had a wound VAC that was placed on his gunshot wound. It helped heal the wound faster and keep the area clean from infection by draining the fluid that would accumulate in the gunshot area. It was interesting to see in person, and frankly, it fascinated me. When it came time to shower, he wouldn't allow anyone to bathe him until I offered. He very reluctantly accepted. When it was time, I would walk him to the bathroom and rinse him. He would try to stand up on his own, even though it was painful, and I never discredited his attempt or asked him to sit. There is nothing more humbling for a human, especially a man like Jake, than to have to accept the help, not because they want it, but because they genuinely need it.

Every time I saw the gunshot wound, the massive amount of bruising, the huge chunk missing from his glute, and the blood being pulled out of the wound, it reminded me that someone tried to kill him. It was hard to comprehend that a complete stranger had tried to kill Jake, my Jake. But they did. They had wanted my husband to die.

The entire time this was going on, I was making a real attempt to stay enrolled in my classes. But that didn't last for longer than a week. I would try to focus on my homework or to sit down and read, but my thoughts would race back to Jake. Eventually, I decided to formally withdraw from all of my courses. After watching him sleep one afternoon, I realized that this would throw off my graduation by an entire year. But at that point, school was no longer my number one priority. I had to get Jake through this.

One frequent visitor that we both became really sympathetic towards was a mother of a patient a few rooms down the hall from us. You could tell that she was worried about her daughter and needed someone to talk to. She saw every young service member on that hospital floor as her daughter. Whenever her daughter was at her appointments, she would come into the room and talk to us.

We would mostly just listen to her talk, but what we managed to find out was that her daughter, only twenty-one years old, had deployed, was blown up by an IED, and was forgotten about by her unit in the hospital. Her chain of command no longer came to visit her, nor did her coworkers. It was definitely not like Jake's unit.

Her unit wrote her off. She had a fiancé as well, but he didn't even come to visit anymore after six months. The next day, when Jake's commander came to visit, he told him about what had happened. His commander was livid. He immediately phoned the girl's commander and tore him a new one, rightfully so. You don't do that to your people. We are family, and family doesn't leave family alone.

I was due to fly back home two weeks after I arrived. I anticipated getting the house ready for Jake, but we later discovered that because of the nature of his injury and the wound vacuum, he would not be coming home. Instead, he would be transferred to Eglin Air Force Base's hospital. There was a weather report forecasting one of the worst snowstorms in twenty years due to hit D.C. only one day after I was scheduled to leave.

I gave Jake a big hug and told him I would be waiting for him at home, but as I started to drive to the airport, the snow started falling. By the time I got to the airport, my flight had been delayed. After I eventually boarded my plane, I realized that I would not be able to make my connection in Atlanta. It was like being in a movie. I grabbed my bag and walked off that plane. I was going back to Jake, snowstorm or not.

I tried to figure out how to take the subway back to Maryland, but the snowstorm had shut down the system. My plan B was to use a cab, but they were no longer coming to the airport because it was too dangerous to drive in the snow. It was getting late, and my last resort was renting a car. I very luckily found the one rental car agency at the airport that had not closed yet and took what I could get.

After whimpering my way through and explaining the circumstances about Jake being in the hospital, I convinced them to rent me a car. Leaving the airport, it really started coming down. There was no one on the roads. Everything was white. When I eventually found my way to the highway, I couldn't even see the lines on the highway. There were cars pulled over on the side of the road that had spun out. I drove down the center of the highway, probably between two lanes, and made my way very slowly back to the hospital, driving about ten miles an hour the entire way.

It was like being in a parallel universe somewhere between *World War Z* and *Mario Kart*. The only cars I saw were abandoned, their lights knocked out. There were no driving lines, and the whole world was bright white. Yet there I was, fighting my way back to the damn hospital. When I finally made it, the gate guards laughed and commended me. I parked the car and ran back up to the hospital room, shaking the snow out of my hair.

As I walked into the room, there Jake was, sitting alone looking out the window. The moment he saw me, he smiled.

I climbed into his hospital bed with him, put my head on his shoulder, and fell asleep. I didn't end up leaving for another week.

We were both getting extremely sick of the hospital room and the food. I was able to track down a wheelchair, and from that point on, I hid the wheelchair in the hospital room so that I could take him out for some fresh air around the hospital daily. Eventually, I got permission from the hospital staff to wheel him across the street to the shopping mall, where they had a full food court.

The first time I took Jake out in the wheelchair, he was angry. He didn't want anyone to see him in a wheelchair. He felt helpless. But Jake can never stay angry with me for more than a few minutes. He refused to let me push him at first until I started cracking jokes about him "rolling through my mind" and "rolling out." After I broke the ice, he let me push him to the mall. We went to a coffee shop and had a mini date at the Panda Express in the mall food court.

During our date, we noticed that there was a younger former Marine two tables away from us. He was missing both legs, and he was sitting with two little boys. After they finished eating, one of the little boys turned and said, "Dad, I want to be just like you when I grow up." He held his dad's hand and walked next to him as he pushed himself in the wheelchair with his other hand.

Jake and I both choked up. Being at Walter Reed enabled me to feel things I had never felt before. It opened my eyes up to a side of this world that is painful and hard to comprehend, but it was an experience I felt grateful for.

On the flight home prior to Jake's transfer, I sat and thought about all the things I had experienced at Walter

Reed. All the faces, the stories, and the impact it had on me, Jake, everything. Life itself is sacred. No amount of money, material possessions, or status can separate you or define you. What defines you is who you are and who you decide to become. What you choose to do in hard situations. The impact you have on others. The story you leave behind when you are no longer on this earth. Jake needed a rock, so I became a rock. Jake needed a nurse, so I became a nurse. Jake needed a friend, so I became a friend.

It was on this flight home that I decided two things:

1. Jake did not need a worried wife right now. Nor did he need someone constantly reminding him that he had limitations and had been injured. He needed to get better, and it was going to be a long time before he was really Jake again. I saw this in the hospital with his irritability. So, I had to figure out how to reach him again and connect with him.
2. I would go to medical school and become a military physician.

CHAPTER 14

Change

I HADN'T BEEN HOME FOR MORE than a week when I got a phone call from one of Jake's team sergeants to let me know what time Jake would be arriving at Eglin Air Force Base. He told me Jake would arrive within the next hour. It was extremely short notice. I quickly stuffed a bag with pillows, blankets, and his comfortable clothes. Then I threw on a coat and drove as fast as I could to Eglin. I wanted to make sure he was comfortable. He had already been in and out of three different hospitals at this point and had no comforts from home aside from me.

I quickly found parking in front of the hospital only to see all of his coworkers, as well as about a hundred other people I didn't know from Eglin, crowding around the flight line, waiting for his transferring aircraft to arrive. Later, I found out the base commander had sent an email out to the entire base, notifying them that a wounded hero was coming home, which, in his defense, was very thoughtful. But it made it hard for me.

I was slightly horrified as I was immediately thrown into a spotlight position as "the stoic and strong controller wife." All I was expecting was a quiet transfer home. When Jake got off the C130, everyone immediately started cheering. Representatives from the public affairs division were there to take photos, and although Jake was smiling, I could tell he was embarrassed by the situation. The fact of the matter was, he didn't want to be here. He wanted to be back with his team, and most importantly, he didn't want to have been shot.

Everyone dispersed, and we were transferred into the hospital where it was just Jake, his team, and me. They all came to see him for the first time, giving him a pat on the back and welcoming him home.

Seeing them interact was always somewhat funny to me. They're a bunch of tough guys, so they really don't show emotion. But when they do try, it is always in the form of a hard slap on the back. You could tell they cared, though. They finally trickled out, and the doctor came in. When he pulled out x-rays and updated Jake and me on the nature of his injury and how close he had come to dying, I choked up. I was exhausted and tired of the constant trains of people, the hospitals, and the nosey wives asking for information because they wanted to be in the know and have something to talk about at brunch. Finally, seeing how close he had come to dying hurt me.

His team doctor explained that the bullet had missed his femoral artery by one centimeter. It not only missed his artery, but it curved around his femur. Had it been any further left or right, Jake would have died. The doctor explained that he did not know how the trajectory of the bullet curved the way that it did and that it was truly a miracle Jake was alive. If it had hit his artery, Jake would have bled out in a matter of minutes.

Although our house was only a few miles between Eglin and Hurlburt Field, I slept at the hospital every night. I would sometimes sleep next to Jake in his hospital bed until the staff would come in and wake him for his check-ups. Most of the time, I slept in a makeshift bed made out of chairs and pillows. Later on, down the line, Jake had mentioned how much it meant to him to still be able to wake up and see me sleeping beside him. It never once crossed my mind to leave his side unless absolutely necessary.

Every time I had to go home to shower and get new clothes, Jake would be up patiently waiting for me to come back. He would tinker on his computer, always keeping one eye on the door for me to pop back in. We would spend a lot of time talking about anything but the hospital. I would bring my laptop, movies, and normal non-hospital food. This made him particularly excited. The hospital food itself was absolutely disgusting, but to have to eat it for as long as he did made it worse. By the end of week one at Eglin, when he knew I was about to leave, he would always tell me his food order. It was the silver lining to being left alone, and it was one of his favorite parts about me returning.

After what we had both seen in Maryland, we knew that this is when a majority of military marriages start to crack—especially if there isn't that strong friend foundation—mainly due to the increase in stress and distance. But we had our way of coping with things. Jake ended up with a small arsenal of funny photos of me in my various sleeping positions by the end of our stay that he would post on Facebook from time to time.

It was at Eglin that they started to wean him off of the morphine and painkillers, which made him extremely irritable and difficult to be around. I could always tell when it was wearing off because he got extremely edgy. It could be anything from the TV being too loud to the nursing staff coming to ask if he was okay. I didn't like it, but I knew what the side effects of withdrawal were. Trust me when I say it is really hard to refrain from snapping back at someone when they're being pissy with you, but I knew that he couldn't help it, and he was still in the recovery process. By me snapping back, we would just end up fighting, which would only weaken the bond we had spent so long strengthening. These are the instances when you have to pick and choose your battles.

When they removed his wound VAC, I was able to bring him home. I pulled up to the front of the hospital in my tiny grey Jetta, and as I looked up, there he was with his cane, walking out. He had refused help from the staff and needed to do it on his own. His face said it all. Jake was mad—not at me, but at the situation. He was mad he got hurt. He was mad he wasn't back fighting with the guys. And he was mad he had to have help in the form of a cane.

When we finally pulled into our driveway, he got out with his cane, walked to the door, set the cane down near our entry hallway, and that was the last time he ever used it.

He walked over to the couch, laid down, and it was quiet for a really long time. I continued on with the household duties and my own life responsibilities, but every time I tried to make conversation, he was quiet and wouldn't make eye contact. I thought he would snap out of it eventually, but the silence only continued.

I would drive him to and from his physical therapist appointments at his unit. It was usually around this point in the day that he would perk up a bit, but after the appointment was over and we were back home, it was the deafening silence again. I gave it a grace period. I figured I would be pretty quiet, too, given the circumstances, and that the amount of life reflection that was probably taking place was going to take some time. But then I started to notice little changes in his personality.

At first, I would notice it in the small things. Things that were out of character for him. Jake was really into mechanical stuff, and he liked working on engines to pass the time or relax. I would leave the house to go grocery shop and run errands, but when I would get back home, he would be exactly how I'd left him: quiet and plugged into whatever Netflix series he could find. I would try to start conversation with him and make small talk, but everything I said to him brought an indifferent response. There was no longer eye contact or smiling. He was there physically, but mentally, he was disconnected, buried in his own mind. This went on for some time until one day, I couldn't ignore it anymore.

"Are you doing okay?" I asked.

He looked at me and snapped, "Do you think I want to be here? All f**ked up?" he yelled. "I should be there right now with my team, and instead, I'm here with a bullet hole in my leg. I can't do anything."

I didn't know how to react. It shocked me. I knew he was hurting, but I was so scared that anything I did or said could tip him over the edge. It was impossible for me to instill feelings of love, support, and concern into his mind for him. So, I decided to give him more time and to continue on with my own life.

After about two months of this behavior and me coming home from school to find him watching episode after episode of *Band of Brothers* from dawn until dusk, I realized there was a big problem. Jake was different now. He had changed. I knew I had to do something and quickly. It was like a floodgate had opened in my mind, and everything was clicking at once. I remembered conversations after deployments with our buddies asking to stay with us, Jonas, the comments, and the personality changes.

I remembered seeing them drinking and crying, talking about their teammates being killed right in front of them, the child soldiers, the massacres of war, their marriages crumbling. That's when it really hit me. The life that was "normal" to me was not the normal world to Jake. My reality was some parallel universe in which all people were good, and there was no threat of anything, except maybe a barista at Starbucks swapping soy for almond milk in my latte.

What he had seen, what he had experienced, was something that good men do because they have to. They do it because if they don't, who will? The sacrifice of self was something I thought I knew, but I didn't quite comprehend until that moment. I knew that if I couldn't reach Jake, if I couldn't find some way of being a friend to him in this time, that our marriage would be over, and he would be lost, like Jonas, forever.

It's more common than you think. You can always see the change in their eyes. It doesn't matter who it is. Their eyes always seem darker after their first deployment. In the harder deployments, the glimmer in their eyes fades. The former way of life is something that they part with very quickly, regardless of whether or not they have a wife and children. This unfortunately had happened about two deployment cycles prior. One of the guys on a different team got back from deployment and up and abandoned his family. He had been married for over fifteen years. Once this type of break happens, they seldom ever reconnect with who they once were, and if they fight it, it's a struggle that isn't easily won.

Some will compare it to having a loved one die. They are physically here. They look the same, they feel the same, but who they once were is dead. That's the hardest thing to accept for many of the spouses that marry these men. The living death of their loved one. I knew that I couldn't expect him to be a husband right now. I knew that if there was one thing he needed, it was a friend. I accepted right then and there that if I couldn't be that for him, I would lose him forever. That week, I was completely unable to sleep. I would stay up at night and hear Jake whimper. I knew I had to try to come up with a game plan.

I knew that if I went to his work, they would slap a PTSD label on his forehead. I also knew that if I did talk to his work, he would resent me. He would be treated differently by his leadership. For as much as I wanted to think the taboo of the PTSD label had changed, it hadn't. It's seen as a weakness. A disability. So, the guys willingly suffer in silence for fear that they will lose a job that has become part of who they are. Jake wasn't the only one going through this. I knew I had to come up with a way to reach him again and connect to his soul, as stupid as that may sound. I also accepted that as of now, I was starting over with Jake. I knew it was not going to be easy. Just seeing what everyone else had gone through and remembering all the relationships before me, I had to accept that there was a chance that I would never get him back again, but I had to at least try.

CHAPTER 15

Numquam Deditionem

THAT NEXT YEAR TURNED OUT to be a complete roller coaster and nightmare. I was working and going to school full-time. Then there was Jake, or what was left of him. I started to drop weight unhealthily fast due to stress and had become frail. Chaplain Smith, whom I spoke to regularly, began to ask me if I was okay and mentioned my weight. I didn't realize how bad it had become.

After his time in solitude came to an end, Jake turned into an angry person. One night we had gone out to the movies, and on the way home, we stopped for gas at one of the small-town gas stations outside of base. It's funny, in the South, time runs like molasses. If something breaks, it usually won't be repaired for some time.

So, we pulled into a gas station that happened to have a broken card reader. Jake blew up, and the situation escalated from zero to sixty very quickly. He started slamming the doors, yelling "F**k this place!" and drove home like a maniac, arguing with me most of the way. At this point, I had had enough with the pity card, and making excuses for him was becoming harder each day.

"What the f**k is your problem?" I said. "You're being an asshole. It's not a big deal. Stop freaking the f**k out, Jake." I was close to a snapping point myself. I had started talking to him like one of the guys. It was the only way that I felt I could get through to him. I had to cut the wife bullshit and the sympathy card. The gloves came off.

"Why is it always an issue with you?" he asked. "It's not me that's the asshole. It's you."

He didn't get it. He was now diverting the problem. I had by now figured out that when he got like this, silence was best. I didn't say anything else. When we walked in the door to our house, he mumbled, "I'm sorry. I don't know why I get like that," and went upstairs to bed.

My inner wife wanted to ignore him and make him sleep on the couch, but I knew he was dealing with something, so these incidences carried on. He would explode. I would push back, correct the behavior, and tell him it was not normal. Then came silence so that he could calm down. Finally, he would apologize.

Some of the time, I really just wanted to walk out the front door and never come home again. Daydreaming about getting away was becoming a daily occurrence, but I couldn't leave him. I loved him too much, and I knew that if the situation were reversed, Jake would do the same for me. By the time summer came around, I had gotten a very random phone call from a girl who I had met a few years back one night out with the guys. She was pretty cool from what I remembered, and we talked every now and then on Facebook. We weren't super close, but definitely more than acquaintances.

She ended up telling me that for a graduation present, her parents were sending her on a trip to Japan. To my excitement, she alluded to the fact that she had an extra ticket, and her parents said they would pay for a friend to go with her. She knew I was into traveling because I had already gone to fifteen countries on my own, so she asked me to go with her. She also told me that she was quietly dating a mutual friend of ours who was stationed in Japan.

Before she could even finish, I blurted out, "Yes!" It was like a marriage proposal. I word-vomited my response. Looking back, I should have probably asked for details, but I was dying for a breath of fresh air and I just wanted to leave. The trip ended up being more of a headache than anything. I found out halfway into the trip that she had lied about dating our friend. They had been hooking up, and she showed up unbeknownst to him. If that wasn't bad enough, it wasn't her parents that had paid for her trip; it was some random older guy she had met on the internet. It became blatantly obvious via a Western Union transfer from a man she called in Atlanta. She was a compulsive liar with no moral compass.

The one thing that did stick with me from this trip was meeting Daniels. He was roommates with our buddy. He knew everything there was to know about me before I could even tell him. The funny thing about social media these days, and especially within this community, is people talk. According to Daniels, I was a very frequent topic of discussion amongst his girlfriend and her best friend…who happened to be the same girl that had gone crazy on Sam. Small world, huh? I'd like to think it was my wittiness, but it was more or less the women in the community that would gossip. Go figure.

Daniels happened to be dating a well-known local. She had been a waitress at a wing place that some of the guys frequented. She was just about as materialistic as they get and completely out of touch with the real world. I had the unfortunate circumstance of meeting her several times out and about. She was the type that would approach you, only to have you quickly run in the opposite direction for fear of losing brain cells when she spoke. Ironically enough, a few years later, she ended up enlisting in the military herself. I'd like to think I was a good influence on her and basically accepted full responsibility for her decision to join. I only did so after I caught her accidentally liking a photo of mine on Instagram, unbeknownst to her.

For the duration of my time in Okinawa, my "friend" managed to repeat her bar-and-ditch tactic nightly. She would sucker me into heading to dinner, then say our friends were meeting up, and proceed to leave with her hookup buddy while leaving me with Daniels. I was pissed, but I think Daniels saw it as an opportunity to open up to me. So, it was in a noodle house somewhere in Okinawa, drunk on snake sake, where I became BFFs with Daniels.

I talked to him about how Jake was different, and he talked about his deployments and how miserable his girlfriend was. We drowned our sorrows in our ramen, completely wasted. I left two days later to catch my flight back to the States. I never spoke to Daniels after that. I don't think he ever spoke to anyone else about what he had been going through or that we were even friends, but I knew deep down, there was a part of Daniels that night that fell for me.

He ended up marrying his girlfriend a few months later, but I don't think she even really ever had an idea about who he truly was. After all, the night before their wedding, she was more preoccupied with trying to bother me out at a bar she had been banned from than focusing on the fact she was actually getting married. The following day, I saw Daniels one last time as he showed up to my house to pick up his groomsman, who happened to be crashing at our house. We didn't talk. By that time, I was far too pissed that I'd had to deal with his psychotic fiancée the night prior and that he would even waste his time with someone that shallow. Some people roll through life with the distractions of material things. People like her don't understand that the best things in life are the people we love.

Shortly after I got back to the States, my Japan "friend" lost her mind when she found out our buddy didn't want to actually date her. She ended up fabricating a pregnancy to try to get him to talk to her. By this point, I realized that she was genuinely crazy and completely cut her out of my life.

As I walked off the plane, I saw Jake. For the first time in a few months, he had actually shaved and looked like he had cleaned up. He even seemed excited to see me, which was shocking because I had already realized I was emotionally disconnected from him. For as much as I was trying to keep it together, the stressors of the deployment were starting to eat at me. We were no longer the happy couple we once were, and to see him excited was actually a shock for me. For as much as I wanted to be happy to see him, I wasn't. I was angry and hurt.

As I transitioned back home, the days became longer, and before I knew it, we were in the thick of summer again. The guys started coming over again, and it was back into party mode, but this time, when we would go out, if Jake drank too much, we always ended up in a fight.

One night, we came home early because he had seen one of the guys he worked with out at the bar. They didn't get along very well, but instead of him dismissing it like he usually would have, he ended up losing his temper, so we came home. He ended up smashing our barstool to pieces. I actually had to call our friend, Tom, to come calm him down. Tom was the one person that Jake was really close to at this point. He too had been through some stuff a few months prior, and his last deployment had been really rough. Tom had seen a few guys on his team get killed. He came home, broke up with his girlfriend of three years, and then hit the booze. It was so sudden; we all knew it was the deployment. It was like he didn't want an attachment to anything in his life prior to that deployment. Unfortunately, his girlfriend was a living reminder of a time that he was trying to forget.

Tom was a heavy-hitter type. Humble and quiet most of the time, but you knew he did good stuff down-range. I called him because I didn't know what else to do. He had been out with us and immediately came over and pulled Jake outside to calm him down. Tom didn't have to say much to me. We already knew what was going on with Jake, but I was starting to shut down. I couldn't handle it anymore.

I couldn't talk to his family because we weren't on good terms. I couldn't talk to his work because they would take his career from him, and that was the one thing Jake actually ironically needed to stay somewhat sane. And I couldn't talk to my family because they weren't there. All I had were my friends and what was left of Jake, but no one really understood what I was going through.

I slept in the guest room that night. Shortly thereafter, little arguments would turn into holes in the walls. Jake never was aggressive to me, but he would get angry, and not knowing how to handle the anger, would turn to our furniture and walls as an outlet. By this time, he became deployable again, which I thought was insane because he was going through stuff mentally at home. The work trips began to resurface again, which was for the best because our relationship had already become unhealthy. We needed the time apart.

I didn't realize how bad it had gotten until my friend Ashley came over to the house. She was the only person that I could talk to because I knew she would keep her mouth shut. She also had been talking to Jameson on and off, so she knew a lot of what I was talking about in regard to the trips and deployments. Sometimes it's hard to talk to civilian friends about the military, especially if they aren't affiliated, but Ashley was the perfect combo. Civilian, but dating military.

We were planning on going out that night to meet some friends for dinner, so she brought her overnight bag. As I was walking her upstairs to our guest room, she whispered under her breath.

"Oh my God," she said. As I turned to look at her, I saw her expression as she looked at me and at the holes in the walls and the holes in my door and the holes in the furniture. I didn't know what to say. "This isn't normal. Are you okay?" she asked. I had become so obsessed with trying to make my relationship work and not giving up that I hadn't realized it had become something I could no longer control and that I had to let go. It broke my heart. I couldn't even cry. I was over feeling mad. I was over feeling sad. I was over it all. I had become just like Jake—empty inside. Each day, we broke more and more, and it had to stop.

CHAPTER 16

The Line in the Sand

BEFORE I MADE MY DECISION, I called the chaplain who had been there with us when Jake had gotten shot. He had known us both this entire time, and I needed some validation to make sure I was making the right decision.

As I sat there in my living room, the chaplain looked at me like I was a kicked puppy. From the time that I had first met him, I had lost over fifteen pounds. It was stress, but at the time, I didn't even realize it. He very delicately explained that I was not the only one going through this, and for as much as I loved Jake, what he was going through was something that I couldn't change.

It was the chaplain that told me what I already knew: Jake was dealing with the emotional pain and trauma of back-to-back deployments. Getting shot was the straw that had broken the camel's back. But the last thing I wanted to hear from anyone was, "God has a plan. Trust him." I broke down into a puddle of tears.

I didn't want God to take Jake from me. Yes, Jake was here in the physical sense. He had ten fingers and ten toes, but he was mentally gone. I didn't want to go with his plan or trust him on this issue. I just wanted Jake. As the chaplain left, I felt a rage wash over me. My mom had called and was trying to convince me to move home, and Jake had even made a few comments about me finding a place to live in Pensacola near my campus. This only made me angrier and drove me deeper into my shell.

Before I knew it, my phone pinged with a text letting me know that Jake had just landed, and he needed to be picked up. As we were driving home, we got into another argument, and I started crying.

I tried in every way possible to tell him how I felt, how to fix it, and what had gone wrong, but after about an hour of talking and seeing him sit there, expressionless, I knew there was nothing more I could do. Then he said, "Listen, I don't feel anything anymore. I'm sorry, but you deserve better."

I felt so angry hearing this that I screamed, "That's it then? Are you f**king kidding me? You f**king robot. I hate you. You gave up. Congratulations, Jake. You f**king gave up on everything."

With that, as much as I didn't want to, I told him he needed to pack his things and move out. I had had Ashley tell Jameson ahead of time what was going on at home. Jameson, the least likely person to become empathetic, especially to something like this, very caringly told me that he would take care of Jake. So, I told Jake he needed to move in with him.

In the past, I had seen other women hold on for dear life to their failing relationships. The only thing that they were truly guilty of a majority of the time was loving their spouses or the idea of what their spouse used to be too much. They didn't understand why the men were different now. It was like walking on eggshells for them, but when you have children, what are you supposed to do? That man is supposed to be your husband, your friend, and the father of your children. So, they hang on with all of their might.

The relationships can turn very bad very quickly, especially depending on how bad the deployment was. So, they fight, hoping that it will change things, but it rarely does. It only forces the two spouses further apart. Typically, the guy will blame his wife for what he is going through. She becomes the root of the problem in his mind, even though, many times, it is the stressors of the deployment. This is always followed by the resentment, the cheating, and the hate. The pain from the deployment doesn't just stop when they come home. Sometimes it manifests in the home. We saw plenty of very messy divorces because of it.

What perhaps many spouses who've come before me never saw was that their other half was hurting, sometimes in a way that we aren't capable of understanding. I didn't want this for Jake and me. I knew what we once had. I knew what we were capable of, so, for the sake of him, I had to let our relationship go. I had to let him go.

Early on, I saw what it was like when relationships died. It was all too familiar with my childhood and I didn't want to repeat that same cycle. I had started praying again, but it was a struggle. I didn't understand why God was letting this happen but what I did know is that, regardless of how much pain I was feeling now, me staying was only going to draw it out.

I drew my line in the sand. I knew what I deserved, and I knew what I was not getting. I could not force Jake to change.

He had to do that on his own. He had to figure out what he was going through and what he wanted on his own. Staying together would only delay the process and cloud his judgment. He couldn't process what he was really going through. It would confuse him. The last thing I wanted him to think was that it was me that was the issue and not his deployments. In both cases, there would be no resolution—not for me and surely not for him.

The day I asked him to move out, we had been upstairs talking. We had gotten into another fight, and I knew this was my time to make peace. I remember it clear as day, telling him that it wasn't working anymore. Jake and I both cried. He knew it was wrong. He knew what he was going through was not normal. And in the middle of our conversation, he broke down.

"I can't feel anything anymore," he said. "It's why I bought that stupid motorcycle when you were in Japan. Nothing makes me happy." He grabbed my shoulders with tears in his eyes, "I don't feel anything anymore."

I was crushed. As he packed his things, all I could do was sit and stare. I was at a loss for words. Life was happening in front of me, but I couldn't make sense of any of it. All of our plans and dreams together ended, just like that, with the closing of the front door. I never felt more alone than I did on that day. I could have been the last person in existence on the planet, and it wouldn't have made a difference.

I had school and would drag myself out of bed in the mornings that week. I don't remember the drives to and from school. I would just sit in class with the worst pit in my stomach. I couldn't focus. I figured if I went to school, it would get my mind off things, but in reality, I shouldn't have. I should have withdrawn. My grades suffered.

I dreaded going home. I couldn't eat. I couldn't sleep. Every night, I would come home to this dark memory and coffin of what was my former relationship. I would cry for hours, sometimes so hard that I would throw up and my chest would hurt. I was truly heartbroken.

By this time, word had spread that Jake and I were no longer together. I would get the occasional text from one of the wives or girlfriends I really had no relationship with, so they could try and find out details. I stopped replying. It was all so fake.

I kept going over what the chaplain said. I stopped answering the phone calls from my parents. I just wanted to be alone. The only person I would talk to was Ashley. Jake texted after the second day of him being out of the house and continued with a long list of excuses:

1. I need to get something from the house. Will you be there?
2. I forgot my beret. I'll be by.
3. Hey.
4. I miss you. I'm sorry how things worked out.
5. You deserve better. (Me: No shit.)

I was so angry with him and hurt that I couldn't even see him without falling to pieces. The moment my phone would go off, my stomach would drop. Finally, by that Thursday, I told him that I loved him very much, but that he hurt me deeply and that there was no way I could have him texting me after everything that had happened. I called a listing that I had found on Craigslist for an apartment for rent, and with that, I told him I would be moving out and blocked his phone number.

CHAPTER 17

The Green Door Saloon

ASHLEY KNEW WHAT I WAS going through, so she and another friend, who was newly divorced, came over that Friday with two bottles of wine. I was like Dr. Jekyll and Mr. Hyde, half of the time laughing when they would cheer me up and the other half of the time in tears. They helped me take our photos off the walls. I tried to hide everything that reminded me of him.

The next day, we decided to go out for dinner on the harbor at one of my favorite seafood places. The reality had set in that we were apart and that I was single again. It was so awkward to even say that word. As we were eating, the table next to us decided to send us drinks. They were older guys, but you could tell they were in shape and well-groomed. I took one look at them and whispered to Ashley that they were Seals. Something about being in the military, you develop a nose for these guys. It's usually the tattoos, the tidy grooming standards, and the watches, but it was definitely what I was picking up on.

Ashley was kind of oblivious to that stuff, although she definitely had a hankering for Jameson. She saw it, more or less, as an opportunity for social interaction and free drinks, so I very quietly sat there staring into my drink while they chatted away. Eventually, one of the guys took notice of my quietness.

"Well, you look pretty upset. What's going on?" he asked.

I think I was all out of tears because typically I would break down if someone asked, but instead, I looked him in the eyes and told him about Jake and everything that had happened. "So that's what's going on." I said.

By the time I was done, he was quiet. There was no reaction. He looked at me and then quickly down, "I'm really sorry to hear that." He was quiet for the remainder of dinner. My story might have affected him. As we wrapped up our meals and called for the check, he leaned over and said, "Why don't you guys head over to the Green Door Saloon with us? We have some friends there. I think you guys would have fun."

Ashley and our other friend agreed. I was just along for the ride. As we walked into the bar, they introduced us to the rest of their team. The shuffleboard table opened up, and one of the guys came up from behind to ask if I'd be his partner. He was tall, had black curly hair, blue eyes, and more tattoos than I could count. Typically, he would have been just my type, but I wasn't over Jake, and I think that everyone in that bar could see that through the façade I was trying to put on.

He grabbed me some of my favorite cider and asked where I was from.

"I'm from LA," I said. "You?"

"I'm a Seal. I'm from Virginia Beach. We're here for the week doing some training over with the guys at the 7th Group," he said. Of course, my luck, the one personality type that I was trying to avoid, I was attracting. He started teasing me about my sad expression. He actually managed to make me laugh, and for a split second, I forgot about everything that had happened—that is, until mid-laugh when I looked up and saw Jake walking into the bar with the rest of his team.

My heart dropped into my stomach. Jake saw me standing next to the Seal and made a beeline for us. This made no sense to me. He clearly didn't want to be with me. He gave up on us, but I could tell that for some reason, he was angry.

"What are you doing here?" he said. "Why am I not surprised to see you out so soon?"

"You're the one who doesn't know what you want," I said. "Besides, you're out too." I almost felt like sticking my tongue out at him, but I held it in.

"Hey, is this guy bothering you?" the Seal asked me.

Jake turned red and clenched his fists. The Seal's entire team came over, and for a split second, it seemed like there was going to be a brawl.

"No, no," I told the Seal, "He's fine. Just an old friend. Excuse me, please."

I grabbed Jake by the collar and dragged him outside to the patio so we could finish the conversation.

"Why am I here?" I yelled. "You don't know what you want. Did you think I was going to sit in the house and cry myself to sleep, like I did earlier this week?" I scoffed. "You can't play games with me. I'm not going to just sit in the house and feel bad for myself. You don't know what you want. That's fine, but I'm not going to sit around and let life happen while you figure your shit out."

As I looked up, I could see Daniels' girlfriend with her band of controller groupies leaning off the edge of their seats to try and hear our conversation. It was hard not to yell that Daniels deserved better and had crushed on me in Japan. I knew it was childish, but at this point, I really didn't care who knew what was going on between us, especially not those bar creatures. Out of nowhere, in front of my newfound shuffleboard partner, Jake suddenly leaned in and kissed me. He grabbed my face and held it firmly. I could feel the desperation and anger in his kiss. The only thing I could figure is that, when he saw me standing next to the Seal, he got jealous.

The one person and personality type that could remotely make Jake feel inferior was another guy of similar stature and job description. Jake had worked with Seals on a few of those deployments and had a lot of respect for them. So, it was the oldest play in the book. He saw me out with another guy, even though we had just met, and became jealous and territorial.

Ashley ran to where we were, grabbed my hand, and dragged me away. Then she called Jameson to come get us. I left extremely upset and so confused. Jameson had become like one of the "girls" with the amount of girl talk we disclosed in front of him. As we drove home and talked about everything that had just transpired, the floodgates opened, and I couldn't control the mess of snot and tears on my face.

Jameson quickly but very softly said, "Hey, you're going to be okay. He's going to be okay too. I'll keep an eye on him, I promise. But you can't let him do this to you anymore." He shook his head, "He's going through some stuff on his own that only he can fix. You have to move on. It's not your fault."

The rest of the drive home was fairly quiet. By this point, I was frustrated with myself that I had even let Jake talk to me. It had ruined everyone's night. As we pulled up to the house, it sank in how unhealthy it was to keep living there. Jake could start over, but for me, staying in the house was like reopening a wound every time I opened the front door. I decided that I was going to check out the apartment I had found on Craigslist the next day.

I looked it up on my computer while everyone else went to sleep. It seemed promising. It was a small one-bedroom right on the water on Okaloosa Island. I wrote down the number to the landlord. Right before I fell asleep, I again went over what the chaplain had said. Up until this point, I prayed before meals, but I didn't openly talk about God with all of my friends. When you're at a low like this, you start doing things out of character and thinking about things you normally wouldn't. It wasn't that I was desperate. I was just coming to new realizations in my life. You can't always control what life has in store for you. Sometimes, no matter how much you fight, there is a different path for you. So, I laid in bed, looking up toward the ceiling, and said, "Okay, God. It's in your hands now. I'm trusting in you to take care of me," and I fell asleep.

CHAPTER 18

Reconciliation

BY THE TIME I WOKE up, Ashley had already headed back home. I called the landlord and made my appointment for one o'clock to go look at the apartment. I was, for the first time in a long time, okay when I woke up that morning. I had accepted the cards that I had been dealt. I knew Jake loved me, but I couldn't force him to change. Only he could consciously choose to address what was going on, and I accepted that. For as much as I didn't want it, we were over. Knowing that I was moving on was relieving. The house was quiet, and my little dog, Jou Jou, was jumping up on my leg for attention. As I picked her up, my phone rang. *Must be the landlord*, I thought and answered it without looking at the number.

"Where are you?" a voice said. It was Jake.

"What do you mean where am I?" I said. "Why are you calling me?"

"Are you at the house?" he asked.

"Jake, I'm getting ready to go look at an apartment in an hour," I said. I should have checked the caller ID. "I'm getting off the phone."

"I'm out front," he said and hung up.

With that, my front door flung open. He didn't even stop to look at me. I was standing at the end of the hall, and he barreled toward me and bear-hugged me. I didn't even have time to react. All I could hear was his truck still running outside and him crying. I didn't know if this was a test or not. I was so mind-boggled over the past year that I didn't trust him. I was still hurt by everything. I knew it was something out of his control. I had seen most of our friends and the guys go through it, but it's different when you're living in the story that everyone is being told about.

It was a very real factor that the gossip among Jake's co-workers was faster than the Internet and that they knew the exact day that we broke up. There was speculation, rumors, and gossip. Some of it was total horseshit, and some of it was closer to the truth, but the fact of the matter was, no one really knew what we were going through or what was going on.

"Jake, sit down," I said. "I'm just about to go look at an apartment. You can't do this to me. It's not fair, and it's hurtful."

"I didn't sleep last night," he said, looking at my face. "After I saw you out with that guy, after I saw you there, smiling with him, it set in. I love you more than anything in this world. I can't lose you. I am so sorry for everything that I have put you through. I'm leaving tomorrow for two weeks for work, but I don't want to go another day without you by my side." He dropped his face into his hands, "I lost myself after I got shot. It's hard for me to even talk about some of the things I have seen and what I have gone through, but you are something that I can't lose. You remind me of who I am and who I was." He looked me in the eye. "I desperately want to be that person again."

I thought back to the night prior, having my moment with God and realizing that I had chosen to trust in what was in store for me. This was exactly what I had wanted to hear for almost a year. I could feel my face get hot, and my eyes watered up. I was so angry with him, yet I knew in my bones I loved him.

"Jake, what f**king guy?" It was starting to bubble forward like a birdbath in the spring, "You mean my shuffleboard partner? I didn't even know him or get his number." It continued to spill out, "I know you didn't mean to, but you broke my heart, and you hurt me. A lot. I don't trust you anymore. How do I know things will be different? I can't just put my life on hold for you anymore." I thought of school and blurted, "I probably ruined my chances of getting into medical school because of all of the shit that happened this past year." I couldn't hold it in anymore, and at that moment, I didn't want to. I wanted the whole world to know what I was feeling. To understand. "I feel alone. I've felt alone for a while," I said, "I can't just run back to you because you're here saying things will be different."

I could still hear his truck running. My nose was a water faucet, and it was like watching a flashback to *The Blair Witch Project.* I went to grab a tissue, "Is your truck still on?" I asked. I walked over to the front door and saw that his truck was still running in our driveway, and his driver door was wide open. He had jumped out of his car to come to me.

He went to turn off the truck and came back in and sat down on the sofa. We talked about everything. The past year, what he was going through, what I was going through. We talked for a long time. I had made a list of non-negotiable terms a while back when we were having big problems. It was a list of things I expected out of someone I loved, especially a husband.

As we sat there, I told him very bluntly, "Jake, this is what I expect if we get back together, and if you can't do any of these things, then you can't have me." No questions asked, he agreed to all, and with that, he pet my head. We were both drained, mentally, physically, and emotionally. But for the first time in a year, I had my best friend back.

"Jake, can we go get fro-yo?" I asked.

"Yes," he said with a short laugh. His hand was still on my head.

He laughed, which was something I hadn't heard in a very long time.

That was four years ago and was the turning point in our relationship. Looking back, I realized my decision to respect myself and draw a line in the sand was the best thing that I could have done for him, me, and our relationship. It was because I made decisions, not out of spite or anger, but out of love and always thinking about what was best for Jake that made a real difference in our progress.

I was able to help many more women after this who were going through the same thing. My experience with Jake and being married to the beret ended up saving more than just one marriage. It helped wives and the girlfriends that came after me—the ones who didn't understand the changes in their loved one and the brave ones who asked for help.

CHAPTER 19

In Loss and War

AFTER EVERYTHING THAT HAPPENED WITH Jake, I was not looking forward to his next deployment. Not only was I still traumatized from him being shot on the previous deployment, but there were so many raw emotions and so much healing that still needed to happen. The job comes first, and before I knew it, he was gone. Again. I was very insecure in our relationship for a while and needed a lot of affirmation as to whether or not he was sure that this was the right thing for the both of us.

Eventually, it subsided with his deployment. I am always adamant about avoiding topics that will distract him from his task at hand. Resorting back to our friend status during his deployments helped alleviate much of what had happened during that year he was home and dealing with getting shot.

Jake had told me during his transition out of country and back home that he had run into our buddy Samson. Samson was taking over Jake's call sign JAG-15. He also held the time record of the quickest yarding-in on his team. He had managed to drink four and a half beers in twelve seconds flat. He was a legend.

Samson and Jake had been pretty tight when he was stationed at Hurlburt Field. He brought out Jake's playful side whenever he saw him. I was coming up on finals in my second-to-last semester and was glad to be done with school and have Jake home. By this time, we were overdue for some "us" time and anticipating announcing to our friends and family that we were actually married and had already been for several years and our plan was to "elope," post a photo, and be done with it. As my mom said, it was very "millennial" of us.

Jake had surprised me by planning a trip to India, and it was there that we were planning to take a photo in front of the Taj Mahal for our elopement announcement. A week before Jake was due back home and I was about to start finals, I was walking to the library on campus when my phone rang.

It was Jake. I could tell on the phone that his nose was stuffy, and there was something about the tone of his voice that set off the alarms in my head.

"Babe, I need to tell you something," he said. In that split second, my mind reverted to the time he had called me to tell me he had gotten shot. I couldn't breathe. "One of our friends was killed," he said. "I can't tell you who it is yet, but he was killed."

My heart sank. Jake was okay, but someone we knew had died. "Is he at your unit?" I asked.

"No. I'll be able to tell you once they notify the family."

"Are you okay?"

"No," he said. I could tell he was close to a breaking point. "I want to come home. I'll call you later. Love you."

"Love you too."

Getting news like that puts the heaviest of weight on your chest and heart. I didn't know who it was, but I knew someone who I considered a friend had been KIA. I was at school and headed to a biology lab. I felt my throat start to knot up. As soon as I got off the phone with Jake, my phone rang again, and it was my friend who had commissioned a year prior and hung out in the same crowd.

"Hey, I need to talk to you," she said.

"Jake just called me," I told her. "Who is it? Tell me."

"Samson's brother happens to be one of my troops. He is at my unit. I just got notification to tell him that Samson's been killed in an ambush. I need your help," she said. My world started to spin. I was thinking about how this would affect Jake. I was thinking about Samson's family and his girlfriend. I was thinking back to a time we were drinking beers and laughing at a bar together. "You cannot tell anyone, okay? Please," she said, snapping me back into reality. "I don't even know if Sadie knows yet." She sighed. "They need help getting money together to send the family to escort his body home. Can you help get something started?"

The tears were already steamrolling down my cheeks. "Yeah, yeah," I said. "I'll do whatever. Let me contact Sadie. I'll call you in a few."

I couldn't attend class that day. I emailed my professor and explained the circumstances. He himself was a Vietnam War veteran and understood what I was going through. A few days later, the Pensacola newspaper published the article explaining what had happened. It was confirmed. Samson was dead.

When I texted Sadie, I could tell she was still in shock. She and Samson had been together for a while, and she had moved from Florida to North Carolina to be with him. I had heard stories of what had happened to the last guy's fiancée when he was killed. She was discarded like an old newspaper, and the community shut her out.

I immediately became concerned for her. Not only did we all just lose Samson, but this was someone that she loved, even if they weren't technically married. I knew how that technicality played out in the career field. As information was released about who had been killed, I continued to be there for Sadie when she needed me. She would usually text very late at night. I knew she was texting when she was alone and missing him. I took this especially hard because of everything that had just happened with Jake. I empathized with her and felt for her.

Jake was still out of the country for a few days before he transitioned home and was asked to speak at Samson's memorial at Bagram Airfield. As he emailed me his speech, and I read what he said, I could feel Jake's pain. This was not just another controller or team guy. This was his friend. Someone he had gone out plenty of nights with and had shared drinks. He was a young, promising, and brave man. Even now, it seems surreal that he is no longer with us. Jake kept that speech for a very long time in his drawer until I eventually put it away in our memory box, deep in our closet.

For a while, everyone and their grandmother were blasting images of Samson on social media. Hurlburt Field held the memorial service, and many units sent guys in who knew Samson and wanted to pay respects. Seeing his family and Sadie up front was hard to watch. By the end of the memorial, there was not a dry eye in the building. Not only had Samson been killed, but so was another guy: the team lead of another team at Jake's STS. It was a memorial for them both.

Sadie was publicly supported when people were watching for the first few months. People would ask for photos with her and post them on their social media. It was painstakingly obvious to see people like Daniels' wife posing with her on Instagram for attention. But after a few months went by, Sadie was slowly pushed out of the community—just as they had all done to the previous fiancées.

Sometime later, I asked her what it was like.

"It's like when a light comes on and the cockroaches scatter," she said.

I knew exactly what she meant. After a while, she was a memory of Samson. She was his girl, and he was now gone. Those who wanted the attention and affiliation at the time of his death now disregarded her, and she was alone. She, just like the rest of us, never had a chance to really say goodbye.

Talking to her one day, she opened up about the connection that they had. She felt it in her stomach the day he was killed, just as I had when Jake had been shot. She loved him deeply and struggled for a long time to move on with her life. People didn't understand and judged her because of that.

When people would bring it up, I would simply say, "I have known people who have loved more in six months together than some do in their entire fruitless marriages." Not many had much to respond to with that. I wish it wasn't true, but the fact remains that this job made me not want to get close to anyone. It was hard to become friends with people, to develop a friendship and, in some instances, love, only to find that friendship and love shredded by the world.

As much as I respected this job, I began to hate it too. I hated what it did to the guys, and to us all. As we sat there celebrating his life at one of Samson's favorite bars, I could see that I was not the only one who felt this way. Then a tray came around with over seventy shots. The room got quiet, and from near his plaque, they said:

> "Here's to the men that wear the beret.
> Not the black, tan, green, or gray.
> But to the maroon and red that we wear on our head.
> Represents the blood that our brothers shed.
> Let us grow old together and never die.
> And we can tell stories of how we used to fly.
> The blood, the sweat, the tears we give.
> First there, that others may live."

The whiskey went down easy and hot as everyone choked their way through the shot. I looked at Sadie, and for the first time, she began to cry. Through the entire time, up until that point, she had been strong. She didn't show her emotions, but it was here that it set in. Samson was gone forever.

It is in those times, in loss and war, that you remember why it is that these men do what they do. It is in these times that we remember how precious life is and how quickly it can be taken away. It is in these times that we remember to kiss our loved ones goodbye and not sweat the small things. In this job, we are reminded that tomorrow is promised to no man.

Samson is still the reigning record holder for the quickest yarding-in. Each man that is lost in war is remembered at every unit with plaques that are nailed up with their favorite items, families, and photos in the halls. They do not die in vain, but are remembered at every function, every day, and kept alive in the memories of every controller and pararescueman that walks the halls of those elite units.

They don't do it for the recognition or for the glamor. Lord knows they don't do it for the money because, frankly, they aren't paid enough. Many don't understand why they continue to go back and at what cost they do, whether it is at a personal loss of their former selves or the sacrifice of their families.

They do it because, in this world, for a good man to do nothing allows evil to prosper. They do it because they are the sheepdogs of our nation. The quiet protectors that will sacrifice anything in a split second, only to laugh in the face of death and prove that this nation is indeed blessed by God.

CHAPTER 20

PTSD

I ALREADY KNOW SOMEONE SAW THIS title and said, "Great, another book on PTSD." Wrong. That's not the perspective I'm coming at you from. There are so many factors regarding these guys, deployments, and PTSD that can't be summed up in some dictionary as a psycho-analyzed term. What constitutes normal, I believe, is the real question. If someone sees something incredibly traumatic, life-changing, or gut-wrenching, it's impossible not to change in some way. Unless you're stagnant in your personal growth as an individual, we are all changing all the time, typically for the better. We are always learning, evolving, and growing. No one ever really stays the same. I know that the circumstances with Jake and I were very different than most. The fact of the matter is war and military love is anything but romantic. You see the constant romanticization of it in movies, but no one sees what really happens to the men and women who come home.

They are treated within the military world, especially in special operations, to be invincible and unbreakable, and they couldn't be more wrong. We aren't immortals. We all have limits. We all change regardless of how much we don't want to think we do. War changes people, and not just physiologically. It reaches down deep to the depths of who we are.

The day Jake came back home after the incident at the Green Door Saloon, he came back to me in mind and spirit. It didn't mean there weren't still things we had to work on. He needed to seriously work on controlling his temper, for one. But that was minimal in retrospect to what he had just gone through emotionally.

A huge problem I have noticed in the military as a whole, as well as in the special operations community, is the taboo mentality that surrounds post-traumatic stress disorder and TBIs (Traumatic Brain Injuries, which typically occur from being in close proximity to blasts and explosions). There was one point in my life, even though I was a military member myself, that I didn't think PTSD was an issue. It wasn't until I observed the changes in the guys that I knew that I really took notice of it. When you are younger, everyone seems invincible, but the fact of the matter is, even the strongest and most courageous of men can be affected by PTSD.

Especially with their operations tempo. Six months home doing training exercises to be prepared to deploy and six months out deployed. Every single year. Some time ago, one of the guys had come back with a TBI and PTSD. It was so bad our buddy had to walk around with a notepad, just to remember things. He would write them down but would still forget meeting times and other details.

The career field ate him alive because of this. He was no longer the alpha. In fact, he was now damaged goods. It's not seen as a result of war; it is seen as a weakness. It is because of this mindset that many of the men go untreated. Our friend ended up getting administratively discharged. This same man dove onto a grenade with a flak jacket to save one of the patients he was working on. It was by the grace of God that the grenade was a dud, but he wasn't even put in for an award because of his previous history. He deserved support and respect from the community, but instead, he was discharged and eventually just faded into the past.

It was instances like that that kept me from notifying Jake's work about what was going on at home. Part of the reason I talked to the chaplain is that I knew he was sworn to secrecy and couldn't disclose any of what I talked about with Jake's work or coworkers. A lot of what I found out, I had come across doing my own research online and observing over the years that I had been in the community. I even eventually got involved with various veterans' organizations and non-profits that helped military members struggling with PTSD.

Everyone, even the guys, has different levels of stress that they can handle before they reach their "breaking points." They all handle it differently. Some bury the memories, only to have them resurface when they are alone. Some turn to alcohol and drugs. Some even turn to suicide. It could happen after one deployment or six. It's rare that you do not see the effect that it has on these men. I can remember so clearly seeing our friends leave on their first deployment and the changes that happen in their faces after six months of fighting. It's always a small, crooked smile to be home, hard swallows when doing toasts, and a glazed, emotionless expression when talking about work.

Historically speaking, this change is not new. In the Old Testament of the Bible, entire cities of refuge were set up for those seeking protection for committing crimes against families of the warring men of Israel because of the immense rage that these men would feel if someone wronged their families. During World War I and World War II, they would call it "shell-shock." If you look at the instances and the number of veterans currently homeless, as well as those in the early '90s and '00s that were Vietnam and Desert Storm veterans, it's no wonder that the military community as a whole has made PTSD such a taboo thing.

So, what is PTSD? To put it simply, humans are designed with two parts of their nervous system which controls normal function. The rest and digest side, or normal function, and the fight or flight response. The fight or flight response is the part of your brain responsible for keeping you alive in times of imminent danger.

When people experience any traumatic event, especially on a repetitive basis, certain parts of their brain become rewired to deal with the stress response. This is why PTSD is not just seen in instances of veterans returning home from war, but it is also seen in many first responders, law enforcement, fire department, and healthcare professionals, especially those working in emergency medical career fields, and even in some instances of abuse, whether it be as an adult or a child.

There is no one book on how to handle PTSD. There is no tell-all blog, diary, shrink, or therapist that can tell you the step-by-step process of how to "cure" someone of it. We as humans are designed to change, adapt, and evolve, but

PTSD is very much a response to an event that greatly impacted someone. The biggest problem I have currently with Veterans Affairs and the military war-machine as a whole is that PTSD is a stigma.

No, you cannot treat someone like an injured dog and expect him or her to get better—especially with the type of men that join special operations. Their job is their livelihood. If you take that away from them, then you are essentially removing part of their soul, but you also cannot deploy men on back-to-back combat-related deployments and not set up the necessary counter-PTSD measures to get these men the help they need.

What I found with many hours of research, listening at veterans' therapy sessions with various organizations, and reading blogs is that the first line of attack from the military and the VA was always medication. There was no way in hell that I was going encourage Jake to get on meds. In fact, there was a higher rate of instances of veteran-related suicide with veterans that were put on antianxiety and antidepressant medication than those that were not. I found this stat via a research paper (*US Pharm*. 2016; 41(11): HS12-HS18.) that had been posted to uspharmacist.com:

> Veterans account for one of every five suicides.[1] Compared to the general population, veterans are less likely to seek care for psychiatric disorders, are more likely to successfully complete suicide, and have a significantly higher suicide risk.[2] In 2014, the Office of Suicide Prevention of the U.S. Department of Veterans Affairs (VA) reported that veterans

> have a 21% higher risk for suicide when compared to civilian adults.[3] Combat exposure to trauma and death are associated with the development of various mental health conditions, such as posttraumatic stress disorder (PTSD) and major depression.[4] Veterans suffering from such psychiatric disorders have up to a 5.7-fold increase in the risk of suicidal ideation as compared to those without.[5] The FDA has identified medications and drug classes with increased suicidality, designating them with black box warnings (BBWs). Addition of such medications to a veteran's drug regimen can further potentiate the risk of suicide.

To me, this translated to, not only did the medication have serious risks, but re-exposure to similar events with conditioning would help relieve the stress response and help the individual to re-learn coping.

I knew what I had to do. I knew and understood what this job was. It is a necessary sacrifice. You may think I am callous for making that statement, but it is true. America is truly a blessed nation, but that freedom, privilege, and way of life come at a great cost.

It comes at the cost of our nation's youth. It comes at the cost of men, like Jake, who choose to stand up against those who would take our way of life, our pursuit of liberty, and our happiness. They are the watchers of our people. They are the silent professionals that take action and wage war in silence, forever ensuring the freedom of our nation. It is these men who fight terrorist organizations, sacrifice their lives, friends, and families, look death in the face, and proceed to tell it to go f**k itself.

Through everything that had happened, all the bullshit, all the deployments, I recalled a conversation I had with my dad, a man of little emotion. His words put it all in perspective for me. "You have tough love. You two will be okay."

So, I did what I knew how to do best. I was a friend to Jake. If I was going to reconnect with him through all of this, I couldn't bitch and complain about him being different. For God's sake, I'm different once a week, once a month, every damn day of the year. Granted, I wasn't going to let him be a dick, but I could at least be this man's friend.

I had grown up shooting with my dad. Shooting was a part of Jake's job, and guns were something he could also tinker with. He is mechanically inclined, and I knew that he would be more than happy to spend all day at the range if I let him, so that became my plan of attack. Jake had gotten shot. He had spent five deployments in combat zones outside of your conventional warfare. He wasn't at the big bases that most military go to. He was with various Green Beret and Seal Teams. I figured if I could take him to the range and change the shooting aspect to something that we would do together, as a sport even, maybe he would calm down. So, I researched competitive shooting and subtly showed him a few YouTube videos one night before bed. He already knew what I was getting at, and he gladly agreed to train me.

I also decided that when he would get mad and blow up, or if I started noticing his heart rate going up, I would pet him. Sounds weird, but when someone you love touches you, your body releases something called cortisol and oxytocin.

These hormones are responsible for making you feel happy and calm. Those hormones would counteract what he was going through with his stress response.

It's important to mention that I wouldn't baby him. He wasn't a pathetic wounded animal. He was a man. I still empowered him. I didn't show pity for him, but I learned to calm him. This was the hardest thing I had to do because initially, he was like a little Sour Patch Kid: super angry and then really apologetic. I chalk it up to God teaching me patience. The first few times at the range, he immediately turned into a team guy with me. I may as well have had a penis with the way he would talk to me. It was complete bro mode at the range, and having your husband turn into your firearms instructor was very interesting, for lack of a better word.

We totally butted heads the first few times. He would yell at me, I would yell back, then he would calm down, and we would do it all over again. Eventually, the days turned into weeks, and our trips to the range turned into routine stops at the gas station for our favorite snacks and a one hour drive out to the range with our favorite playlist. And after two months, it turned into something we were looking forward to doing every weekend.

The range was never too crowded. It was somewhere he felt comfortable. He could have his time to quiet his mind. You wouldn't think that shooting would be something that would be quiet, but when you become extremely focused on a competitive goal, your mind quiets.

Once we started shooting, our connection came back very strongly. It was the range that brought us together as friends again. Once that was re-established, and he knew he could talk to me without me judging him, we could focus on being husband and wife again. It is my belief that it was our friendship that kept us together during one of the hardest parts of both of our lives. I didn't just love him as a significant other—I cared for him genuinely as a friend.

I realize that this is not the circumstance for all women who have been with men who have seen war. Like I said before, everyone handles it differently, but I can say that had I stayed and let him unintentionally take out his feelings on me along with forcing him to be with me, he never would have had time to reflect and truly see what the real issue was. I had to make the decision to continue living, even if it meant without him, to save him and what was left of our relationship. This is why it is so important for the women who love these men to always be able to stand on their own.

We cannot control what happens in love and war. We cannot make someone change back to who they once were after they have seen some of the traumatic things that war exposes the human soul to. We many times are only shown a small part of these men, the parts that they want us to see. Sometimes we have families with them, but they come home different. We don't ever stop loving the man they once were. Sometimes they come home, but not mentally.

Don't ever think there was anything you could have done differently. I have seen so many nasty divorces simply because the women do not understand. They think that the men are intentionally being distant and cut off instead of realizing what they are going through and trying to see why the divorce is happening. Don't be like those women. Go in peace, for your own soul. Fight like hell to help them. Don't turn your back on them. But know when it is time to let go. You never know the outcome of what will happen in these circumstances, but one thing I do know is when you truly love someone and they truly love you, the love you share will always come back to you.

Am I a doctor yet? No. Do I understand that the human mind is far more advanced than we know? Yes. The mind is capable of rewiring itself, which means that the mind is also capable of healing itself. The one issue I came across working with various PTSD nonprofits is the amount of psychotropic medications that are dispensed to those suffering from PTSD. During group therapy sessions that I attended for some of these nonprofits, many of the veterans talked about service animals, CBD oil, and meditation helping.

Knowing what I know now about Jake, a pill would not have helped him. I didn't want him to be medicated and doped up. I would not change a thing that I went through or what happened between us, knowing what I know now. Jake can now talk to me, after almost nine years together, about some of the things he has seen. It's not always easy seeing him talk about these things. Sometimes it happens randomly. It could be a song, children playing, us driving, but I'm always there to listen, and I do believe that is the most important thing. You cannot carry a burden like war alone.

CHAPTER 21

Put Your Big Girl Pants On

YOU'LL GO THROUGH A LOT of shit when dating or marrying one of these guys. The deployments, the training cycles, managing the home, being a part-time single parent, the gossipy circles, financial strain, emotional hardships. The list goes on and on. It's pretty much endless. I can say that, as a military member, it was even harder at times because the military comes first, always. However, looking back at some of the women I have met, my heart goes out to them, which is why I wrote this book.

The ones able to last the deployments and the hardships that come with them, the ones who live by tough love. As my dad would say, they embody the strong Spartan wife—the wife who can stand on her own, doesn't feel sorry for herself, and doesn't loathe in self-pity for the situations that are thrown her way. Of the countless marriages, breakups, and divorces I've seen, it was only a select few women who managed to maintain the home life while balancing military life and maintaining a healthy relationship with their husbands.

You have no idea what is going on in anyone's relationship at any one point in time. Someone can appear to have the ideal relationship, yet there could be affairs happening left and right, secret drug use, or a horrific home life. I have gotten many phone calls over the past several years from women that were either dating or married to one of my husband's coworkers. It usually is the same questions and thoughts.

"I don't understand why we're fighting," they say. Or, "He's acting different." Sometimes it's, "He has a temper." Or maybe the worst, "He doesn't want to commit."

I always give them the same advice:

1. DO NOT be a doormat. If you have a problem, vocalize it. No one is born psychic, so how the hell are they expected to know what is bothering you if you don't say anything?

2. For the first thirty days after a deployment, your significant other is going to take time to adjust to "normal" life. Not only will his heart rate be elevated, but he's going to need time to mentally adjust back to what we know as normal. The absolute worst thing you can do is bring him out drinking to noisy locations. Let him adjust at his own pace.

3. Make sure you always have your own life. By that, I mean, do not live through your husband and his career. It is okay and healthy for you to have your own

friends, career, and extracurricular activities. In most cases, it will actually help the relationship because it not only will keep you busy during long deployments and work trips, but you will feel content being able to contribute to the marriage. The number one problem that I constantly see happen with women is the fact that they do not branch out. They live and breathe their husband's job. You can be supportive and have your own life at the same time.

4. <u>If he doesn't want to commit, ask yourself why.</u> You cannot force anyone to marry you or stay married to you. You cannot get pregnant and expect it to be a fix-all to existing marital or relationship issues. Also, don't rush into getting pregnant to solidify your relationship. Mark my words: they will change. Either you evolve together, or the relationship ends. Kids will only complicate things, and in many cases, it still ends in divorce. If you sit around waiting for commitment and are putting out, guess what? You're probably not going to get it. I saw this happen scores of times. You should not play the dick-dick game where you're not wanting to text for fear of looking clingy or not calling because he is supposed to call first. If a man wants to be around you, he WILL move heaven and earth to do so. If you are with someone who is not giving you the time of day, it's because you're not a factor in their life. Move on.

5. <u>Be you.</u> You cannot lie your way into a relationship, and that is the worst foundation for a marriage ever. Eventually, after the honeymoon phase is over, you

begin to realize who it is you actually are with. Why start off pretending to be someone you're not? It will only end in disaster. Be the genuine you. If they don't like that, they're not the one intended for you. When you meet the right person, you will just click. It won't be complicated, and it won't take energy from you. It will make you happy to be alive. Don't settle for less. If you have standards, then keep them.

6. Get a good deployment friend. This can be any woman, preferably one who has a significant other in the military, that will understand the acronyms, the deployment jargon, and will understand when you're saying that you are worried because you haven't talked to your loved one. The last thing any wife or girlfriend wants to hear is, "You know what you signed up for."

7. Try not to go out and party while your significant other is deployed. This always baffled me, especially after Jake got shot. It's not a good look, for one. But God forbid something happens. Do you really want to have the fact that you were out wasted on your conscience? Even more so, don't latch on to his friends or coworkers. Not all men are created equally, and you don't want to put yourself in a situation where you could jeopardize your relationship while your significant other is deployed.

8. And the last, most important rule: If you end up in the same circumstances I did, don't lose your mind. Stay away from his friends. Give him space and time. Keep

your head on tight, and as hard as it is, move forward in a classy and peaceful fashion. If it is meant to be, he will find his way back to you. If it's not, there will be someone better out there for you.

CHAPTER 22

My Advice to You

Everyone knows who the Spartans were. They are, historically, the most glorified and badass ancient Grecian fight force that went down in history for fighting the Persians at the Battle of Thermopylae. A little-known fact about them: It was not just the men who were judged on their physical strength and mental agility. Their society was founded on the character and strength of their women too. These women were expected to have the same physical training and education as the men. The idea behind it is that a strong woman raises a strong man, and those men, in turn, would fight wars.

Think about that for a moment. The greatest military ever assembled, the most elite fighting force, was based on the strength of the women they loved. Do you think these women felt sorry for themselves? Do you think they were able to maintain their homes and rise to the occasion when things happened and their husbands were gone? Absolutely. They were strong in character. They knew sacrifice, dedication, and loyalty. They were known among the ancient Greeks as being independent and strong.

These are the women you need to think about when you marry into the military community, especially into the special operations community. If you want your relationship to last, you need to embody the strengths that these women had. One of the most heartbreaking stories I have ever heard was about a nineteen-year-old Marine that had been deployed in the Helms Province in Afghanistan. He hit a roadside bomb with his convoy and lost both legs and part of his right arm.

It was his first deployment, and he was newly married to a girl he had met a few months prior around Camp Lejeune in North Carolina. When the family liaison of the hospital went to the airport to pick her up, she didn't show up. When they contacted her several more times, she eventually wrote an email stating that the situation wasn't something she had "signed up for" and sent him divorce papers.

The deployments, the injuries, the operations tempo. It tests any relationship and/or marriage. A majority of the time, it chews them up and spits them out. In times like these, remember, you cannot, and absolutely should not, ever give up on your spouse—unless they are choosing not to get help, in instances of PTSD, and you are finding yourself in a physically and emotionally dangerous situation.

Know when you marry one of these men, there is a very real possibility that this person may get hurt, and one day, you will probably lose someone you know. It pains me to have to say this, but some people don't understand the harsh reality of this job. They don't realize that they may not deploy to a safe location and may not come home one day. I really never did understand the wives and girlfriends that would be out partying while their husbands and boyfriends were away. Maybe it was because they didn't understand what they were seeing or didn't know what was really happening. Once you accept that, a lot of little annoyances will suddenly become irrelevant in your life, and in my opinion, your relationship will actually get better.

Respect your relationship. Learn to keep it private. For as much as the community is like a family, at the end of the day, it is where your significant other is going to work. Cardinal rule number one: Thou shall not be messy on social media or speak ill of your husband/boyfriend to his coworkers or affiliates. I would not be saying this if it didn't actually happen. It is okay and recommended to not air out your personal business to the world.

Respect one another, ladies. Do not alienate other women. Fact: You will not get along with everyone you meet, but you can learn to respect one another. This should be done for a few reasons. First, it will cause problems for him if you are beefing it with his teammate's girlfriends or wives. Secondly, there will be times in your relationship where you will be able to find out more about what is going on with the deployments, homecomings, work trips, and military events from the other women who are in the community.

When younger women come into the community, do not alienate them. Mentor them, help them, and be a sister to them. Do not put yourself on a pedestal because you are a "wife" and they are a "girlfriend." I have seen more loveless marriages after a few deployments than some of our friends who have been dating for five years or more. You will hear gossip, you will see things happen, and you will have the choice to either continue spreading that dirt or to not. Leave the drama out of his work environment. You are a reflection of him. Do you really want him to be looked down at? **ALWAYS** take the higher road.

Cut him some slack with communicating when he is gone for work. Do not bring up insignificant problems when he is deployed. Remember that it is important for him to be in a good mental state when he is doing what he is doing. Stressors at home can very much so affect his work performance, and the last thing you want is for him to be worrying about things at home when his life is on the line.

Know that you are the backbone of your relationship. There will come a time when he will need you more than you could have ever imagined. Know that he is very brave and strong, but even the strongest men can cry. It doesn't mean they are weak. It means that they have a soul.

Don't get too bent out of shape about dates. Vacation dates will be almost impossible to schedule, birthdays and anniversaries will be missed, and at some point, you will attend a special event, like a marriage or graduation, alone. It's not his fault. You married him, and with that comes the United States military.

Lastly, if there is one thing you take from this entire book, it should be never stay angry. What I have learned about being in this community over the last ten years is things change at a moment's notice, and this job, along with life, will throw you constant curveballs. It is not worth regretting things that you could have or should have said.

At the end of all of this, you will look back, and it will seem as though it went by in the blink of an eye. The days will all blur together, and before you know it, he'll either be getting out or retiring. Remember, life is short, and when we leave this earth, we cannot take material things with us. Only the memories from loved ones and the impact we had on people's lives remain.

So, stay strong, stay brave, and stay free. And always remember that the life you're living is at the sacrifice of another's.

GLOSSARY

ADAPT: Alcohol and Drug Abuse Prevention & Treatment

AFSOC: Air Force Special Operations Command

AWOL: Absent Without Leave

CBD: Cannabidiol

CCT: Combat Controller

CCS: Combat Control School

CTO: Commander's Time Off

IED: Improvised Explosive Device

KIA: Killed in Action

MARSOC: Marine Corps Forces Special Operations Command

Paperwork: Military administration disciplinary action

PC: Permanent change (of duty station). Moving to a different base

Pipeline: Combat Control and Pararescueman training school, about two years long.

PJ: Pararescueman/men

PTSD: Post-Traumatic Stress Disorder

Schoolhouse: Training location while new Controllers and PJs are going through the pipeline.

SGLI: Servicemembers Group Life Insurance

STD: Sexually Transmitted Disease

STTS: Special Tactics Training Squadron, aka "the schoolhouse"

STS: Special Tactics Squadron

STU: Special Tactics Units

TBI: Traumatic Brain Injury

TDY: Temporary Duty

VBIED: Vehicle-Borne Improvised Explosive Device

ABOUT THE AUTHOR

Anna Paulina Luna is an Air Force veteran who joined the Air Force at age nineteen. She spent a total of six years in the military, including five on active duty. During her time in service, she was awarded the USAF Achievement medal. She is a small business owner with a degree in biology from the University of West Florida. She is a producer, media personality, and political commentator. Anna currently resides in Florida with her husband and two dogs.